Tradition and Change

TRADITION AND CHANGE

The New American Craftsman

by Julie Hall

Foreword by Rose Slivka, Editor-in-Chief, *Craft Horizons*

E. P. Dutton   New York

To the American Craftsman

(Frontispiece, page 2). *Midnight Masquerade*. Patti Warashina. 1977. Low-fire ceramic with underglaze. H. 28″; W. 18″; D. 14″.

Contents

Acknowledgments

This book, like many extended and complicated undertakings, was completed with the assistance and cooperation of a number of people. First and foremost I should like to acknowledge the many craftsmen who shared their photographs and other records. I especially thank them for their patience during the exchanges of letters and phone calls that sometimes seemed endless.

I should also like to thank the following individuals who gave special support and help during the writing and preparation of this book: Robert Bishop, Sylvia Brown, Ned Crouch, Michael Hall, Wayne Higby, Marvin Lipofsky, Cyril Nelson, Rose Slivka, Lorraine Wild, Nancy Yaw.

Foreword

The last thirty years have seen the creation of the modern craft history of the United States, and with it the most remarkable phenomenon of our time—as challenging as the space age, as penetrating as computer technology—the birth of a handcraft culture sprung from the very heart of our industrial society.

Today the handcrafts and the fine arts of this country enjoy a relationship of energies unique to the United States. The new creative sensibility of our time is infused with the spirit of handcraft. It is not a renaissance, it is not a revival, it is not a rebirth. It is a brand-new phenomenon—a handcraft culture feeding into and fed by industrial freedoms—along with modern painting and modern sculpture.

Modern handcraft would not have been possible without the machine to free the craftsmaker to make individual choices, without the accessibility to the cultures of the world, and without the presence of modern painting.

In contrast to Europe and Latin America, North American craftsmakers never made objects for a ruling class, the church, or the court: they made craft in and for an egalitarian society. They learned their skills in the workshops of the universities or professional schools, in an environment of fellowship and camaraderie where energies and enthusiasms ignited each other, where there were no secrets of technique and materials, where knowledge was exchanged and discoveries were shared, where the secret was in the unique imprint of individual personality, not in virtuoso techniques, although technical innovations abounded in every direction and combination.

Craft and art join in erasing lines and distinctions that the choice of materials and techniques heretofore imposed, maintaining an outworn hierarchy of forms and functions. The concerns with ideas, energy, irony, mystery, traditionally the realm of "fine art," are equally the concerns of modern craft. Art crosses over into craft, liberating and celebrating materials, bringing attention to function and method.

Each craft object reveals its making and reflects the temperament, intellect, and skills of its maker. The abundance and accessibility of materials, new and old, have further contributed to the disappearance of barriers. New media, in particular, having escaped being appropriated and categorized as belonging either to the crafts or the arts, provide a common aesthetic ground.

Both functional craft and artcraft have mutual aesthetic and practical concerns. Both need each other and nourish each other, for the art of the modern craftsmaker is to transform life into things and things into life.

Rose Slivka

May 27, 1977

Preface

This book was conceived with several objectives in mind. The principal aim was to compile a clear pictorial survey of the most exciting and influential work being done in crafts today. The pictures, of course, speak for themselves and should stimulate an appreciation for the craftsman's ongoing contribution to American culture. The text was intended to link the images in the photographs to a sense of history. A thread of tradition weaves subtly through the contemporary craft scene and has been traced here to its several sources. Finally, the book attempts to interpret crafts as an art form and to clarify the views and values of the talented innovators in the field of crafts today. Many fine books and exhibition catalogues dealing with the crafts precede this effort. They provided the foundation for this particular survey, which, in its own way, seeks to extend and update the critical dialogue that is always necessary in any area of the arts.

The first outline of this book was constructed around traditional craft processes and materials. All clay objects were grouped in a section on "pottery" and all fiber works in a section called "weaving," etc. The precedent for this is widespread and accepted by most authors writing on the crafts, and also by curators seeking formats for exhibitions of craftwork. After visits to studios all across the country and after dozens of interviews with working craftsmen, this author came to the realization that the expression of the contemporary American craftsman is a subject far too complex to be interpreted in a survey based on materials alone.

Across media boundaries there is, for · example, a strong affinity between the work of Paul Soldner, a potter, and that of Trude Guermonprez, a weaver. Both of these artists have strong "craft" backgrounds using the traditional tools of their respective disciplines. Both have an almost classical interest in the human figure as a motif in their work. Both are sensitive to the subtleties of Japanese art and reflect this influence in their own art. This discovery that certain common values, approaches, and motives could link a weaver's art to that of a potter opened the door to the structuring of a new kind of book on the crafts. One at a time the chapters in this book evolved as a means of probing the intrinsic qualities of the craftsman's art.

The chapter groupings here that point up similarities between artists by no means overlook the important differences between them. All artists express a great deal more in their work than can be indicated by even the best generic designations. It should always be kept in mind that Monet as an artist was never limited by the appellation, "Impressionist." In this same sense the labels applied here are intended to illuminate rather than to restrict the art of the American craftsman.

Who should be included in a book with the word *craftsman* in its title? This question initially caused considerable confusion, which was quickly resolved as the book took form. Craftsmen ultimately are recognizable as a special group of creative people with their own identity, their own history, and their own unique art expression.

Almost all craftsmen, early in their training, put in many long hours learning to master the loom, the blowpipe, the potter's wheel, the wood lathe, or the array of hammers and stakes needed to form hollow ware. This orientation contrasts markedly with that of artists trained in stretcher making, oil painting, armature building, and figure modeling. The role of training in the craftsman's identity is well illustrated through a comparison of glassworkers, Harvey Littleton and Larry Bell. Both men work in the same material and both are certainly artists. Only Littleton's background, however, is strongly rooted in the crafts. During his childhood years he spent many hours watching glassblowers at the Corning Glass Works where his father was vice-president and director of research. Later, he himself spent many years working as a potter before turning to the glassblower's art. Bell, on the other hand, was trained as a painter and comes from what is generally referred to as a fine arts background. He arrives at his use of glass essentially as someone translating the precepts of Cubism and Constructivism into transparent materials.

Of the two, only Harvey Littleton is comfortable with the label "craftsman." He has fathered an entire generation of American glassblowers who have become integral and identifiable parts of the craft community. Littleton, not Bell, was the influence that brought a consciousness of the creative potential of glass to the American craft world.

Craftsmen are, for the most part, an interrelated professional community. Despite any quarrel over the label "craftsman," they interact through workshop programs that move them across the country lecturing and teaching. They know each other's work through periodicals and journals focused exclusively on the crafts. They share a common system of galleries and a growing number of museums committed to exhibiting their work, and they acknowledge one another in a very particularized environment that is the craftsman's world. Selecting the artists to be included in a book on crafts was not difficult, for they essentially selected themselves.

The most pressing editorial responsibility inherent in the formulation of a book on crafts today is the attempt to resolve the unnecessary confusion that often results from the usage of the words *art* and *craft*. Most craftsmen do not want to feel that their best efforts cannot stand as *art*. Art in a broad sense can be defined as any aesthetic insight made manifest through a creative shaping of materials into form. This definition makes it obvious that craftsmen have fashioned art from all manner of craft materials, using so-called craft processes throughout all time. Craftsmen today approach art through disciplines rooted in tradition and that persist as ongoing attitudes toward particular processes and materials.

One of the primary frictions in the contemporary art versus craft debate revolves around the issue of function. The prevailing notion is that crafts are utilitarian, whereas art is born of pure aesthetic motives unencumbered (and untainted) by functionality. Consequently, there is pressure on the craftsman on every side to abandon the making of anything functional in order to prove that he or she is involved in the making of art. This pressure is totally unjustified in the face of history. Is a carved chief's stool from the Congo art or craft? Is a decorated Greek urn fine art or decorative art? Both the stool and the urn were used, but both have found their way into art museums and art auctions as certified works of art.

Pulled out of time and context, the functional aspects of the stool and the urn have been obscured. Unfortunately, the modern appreciation of these two objects, which is based in a perceptual set rejecting or conveniently ignoring their prior functions, becomes both too sophisticated and too naïve to be complete. The urn in the urn remains no matter what. And so the true aesthetic issue must turn to a measure of the beauty in the urn, and this is where the artist in the craftsman who made the urn is to be found

or not. Today's craftsmen are asking critics and collectors to approach their contemporary functional objects as art and to evaluate them aesthetically in a context that does not require an erasure of the services they can perform on another level.

The prevalent notion that a true work of art is inherently unique in form also frequently undermines the art credibility of objects created by craftsmen, particularly those working on forms in series. Real art, however, eludes this limit and indeed sometimes comes from the most repetitious approaches to the development of a visual idea. Alberto Giacometti's claim to the title "artist" has never been challenged on the grounds that he spent too many years making the same thin, standing figures over and over. In a similar vein the art in Momoyama period Japanese pottery has never been depreciated by some negative coefficient based on the similarity of forms found in all three-gallon storage jars produced at the Tamba potteries. Serially produced objects do not necessarily lack resourcefulness, impact, or beauty. The best contemporary craftsmen, like most artists, seek the specific, the meaningful, and the universal in all the forms they create.

Critics and connoisseurs today are developing a broader understanding of art and craft and how they relate to each other and to man and culture. A most impressive affirmation of this fact was offered by the National Gallery of Art in Washington, D.C., in its 1974 exhibition entitled "African Art in Motion." In this exhibit beautiful, carved wooden masks were conventionally presented on pedestals. As static "art" objects they were far removed from the hands of the tribal artisans who skillfully fashioned them in conformity with traditional designs passed down through the generations. Behind the masks, however, the museum curators presented a series of continuous film projections that documented African dancers "using" the masks in ritual dances. The films showed the masks encompassed by wild manes of raffia atop brilliant woven costumes, pulsing and throbbing in kinetic concert with the rhythmic motions of the dancers' bodies. Here was African art shown both in a "pure" form and in the context of a functioning craft reunited with its African craft genesis.

Articulating the key problem currently preoccupying American craftsmen, potter Paul Soldner once said to the author, "When we [craftsmen] get a pot in the Whitney [Whitney Museum of American Art], then we will really be somewhere." This end is in sight today. The persistent hard work and ambition of craftsmen like Soldner and the insights evolving out of exhibitions like "African Art in Motion" will bring it all about. But beyond breaking down old biases and restructuring definitions, one other challenge persists for all craftsmen. In the final analysis the things they make must stand on their own in the broad stream of art history. Art is one of the most difficult things to identify. Finding the real art among the numerous object in today's art world is very taxing, no matter what the objects are labeled. The mystique of art allows artists, dealers, and museums to put a lot of things on pedestals, wrap them in lengthy dialogue, and pronounce them to be art. Today's art audience viewing so many things dressed in such fine rhetoric often feels as though it is looking at the emperor's new clothes and wonders if indeed there isn't a lot of nudity around.

Art exists. It exists in many forms, some of which command high prices in the marketplace and some of which are given away. Finding out what is art is a lifelong search even for artists. The search for art is not rooted in semantics, which polarizes art and craft. Art criticism today needs a word that means "artlike but not art" to differentiate what may truly be art from its many look-alikes. A complex process that is fundamentally democratic sifts through the art milieu of any culture and in time finally elevates certain things to the level of masterpieces and certain artists to the level of masters.

Much of the work in this book is illustrated for the first time, beginning a bid for acceptance that cannot be concluded here. Many beautiful objects are illustrated between these covers, and certainly time will identify some of them as masterpieces. In the interim, however, it is hoped that the book can also illuminate the moods and motives of contemporary American craftsmen as they seek to merge tradition, change, feeling, learning, and self-realization into forms of art. This book attempts to analyze, describe, and interpret a broad range of artistic objects created by a vigorous and diversified group of artists. This book is dedicated to these artists and endeavors to establish some guideposts that will extend an appreciation of their art to an ever-widening audience. If the ideas and images in this book serve to stimulate new thought on the subject of American crafts, then the book will have accomplished a worthy purpose in the service of its principal subject, the new American craftsman.

Introduction

American crafts, like all things American, have undergone tremendous changes in the last twenty-five years. Some traditions have been sustained while others have been cast aside in favor of innovation. Putting today's crafts in focus requires a brief look at a craft history, beginning, like America herself, in England.

Throughout the nineteenth century, the rush of industrialism threatened the extinction of handicrafts in most of Western Europe. At mid-century a cry of alarm had been sounded by both the Scottish historian, Thomas Carlyle, and the English social critic, John Ruskin. Another Englishman, William Morris, picked up the alarm and became the father of what was called the Arts and Crafts Revival. Morris, an energetic poet, artist, social theorist, and romantic visionary, decried the loss in the quality of life in the soot-blackened cities of his native land. His message was timely. It had impact throughout the Continent as well as finding acceptance in the United States.

Morris's romantic side projected a return to an idyllic world where people lived in perfect rustic harmony with their environment and remained in close touch with their craft traditions. His romanticism, however, was tempered with the practical understanding that modern craftsmen would have to face a certain separation from the forms and values of their preindustrial forebears. He knew that this separation resulted from the inevitable advance of the machines that had destroyed the old ways. Writing his thoughts in a preface of the book *Arts and Crafts Essays* (1899), he stated:

. . . our art is the work of a small minority composed of educated persons, fully conscious of their aim of producing beauty, and distinguished from the great body of workmen by that aim.

In America, as in England, the preindustrial craft heritage had almost totally disappeared by 1900. The westward movement and the expansion of urban industry severed American culture from its native Indian and early Colonial craft roots. The turn of the century found a few American craftsmen experiencing the dissolution of their traditions with a great sense of loss. Following the lead of the English, they began to revitalize the craft forms that could be adapted to modern American life.

Foremost among the American pioneers was Louis Comfort Tiffany. He spoke eloquently for the placement of well-designed and carefully crafted objects within the American home. By 1910, he was training American craftsmen as apprentices at his renowned glassworks. Tiffany was a master designer who insisted upon impeccable craftsmanship in all phases of production, and he was especially attentive to that aspect of his studio which concerned itself with the fabrication of decorative leaded glass windows and lamps. His designs incorporated the forms of American flora and fauna into curving entwined patterns. The Tiffany expression of the Art Nouveau style became the hallmark of the period and the name Tiffany, the eponym for Art Nouveau. Louis Comfort Tiffany, craftsman, was in every sense a modern man with a modern view and a solid understanding of modern business. His finely crafted leaded glass, wood, and metal fixtures created a craft consciousness in America that continues to the present day.

Any process that can be correctly called a revival is of necessity a conscious and directed process. The revival that created a place for the crafts in modern America was no

1

exception. As Morris had predicted, and as Tiffany had proven, the future of crafts depended on the sophistication of twentieth-century craftsmen. The peasant craftsman serving the community with the skills of a family trade was no more. The history of modern crafts became a complex history of artists, ideas, and concepts of expression.

From the fountainhead of revivalism came a flow of energy and vision that has established and sustained two distinctly different, but equally sophisticated, streams in the history of modern American crafts. One flows directly from Morris's notion that traditional functional crafts can still be profitably produced by hand in an era of mechanization by craftsmen who find pleasure in the rhythms of a simple life of work and service. The other drifts away from the production of useful crafts and runs toward the challenges that faced Tiffany and others of his generation in attempting to fashion all manner of unique and decorative craft objects.

As World War I ended, the future of American crafts was still being shaped in Europe. The German Bauhaus became the international hub of thought on the aesthetic problems of modern living. This famous school-workshop was a laboratory where an entire generation of sophisticated designers and craftsmen sought to integrate architecture, sculpture, painting, and crafts. Bauhaus philosophy was highly optimistic about the utilization of machine-age tech-

2. Carved and painted chest of drawers with applied split spindles. Attributed to Thomas Dennis. Dated 1678. W. 44¾". (The Henry Francis du Pont Winterthur Museum, Winterthur, Delaware)

3. *Prayer Rug.* Loja Saarinen. Woven by Valborg Nordquist. 1928. Wool. 67" x 52½". (Cranbrook Academy of Art Museum, Bloomfield Hills, Michigan)

3

nology to serve man's purpose of enriching and humanizing every visual aspect of the modern world. The Bauhaus ethic evolved into a style expressing rationality and functionality through clean lines and strong rectilinear design motifs. Bauhaus purism eclipsed the appeal of Art Nouveau for both European and American craftsmen and provided them with forms and ideas that led to the production of textiles, furniture, ceramics, and metalware designed for the flawed, but potentially fertile, affluent modern world.

The postwar spirit of internationalism in the crafts touched America in the late 1920s with the establishment of several important craft schools and societies. The Cranbrook Academy of Art in Bloomfield Hills, Michigan, typified this movement. Under the direction of Finnish architect, Eliel Saarinen, Cranbrook was a small community of painters, sculptors, weavers, bookbinders, and metalcraftsmen assembled from Europe and America. In the 1930s American craftsmen like those at Cranbrook succeeded in synthesizing the organic and geometric forms of modern European crafts into a style later to be called Art Deco. The deco style merged rich ornamental natural forms with bold simple shapes, and at Cranbrook it found expression in textiles and metalwork as well as in architecture and furniture design. Cranbrook evolved into a major art school where teachers like Finnish potter Maija Grotell distinguished themselves as leading forces in American crafts, both through their own work and through their influence on the generation of young craftsmen who studied under them.

4

In the period between the two world wars many American art schools began to incorporate craft courses in their curricula. For the first time, schools began to assume the role of patron for craftsmen and to employ increasing numbers of them as teachers. The craftsman-teacher emerged in the 1930s as a craftsman with a new kind of freedom to explore art expressions divorced from the economics of production and sales. Young craftsmen seeking training began to seek art schools and universities, rather than the traditional apprentice system, as the arena for testing new ideas in all areas of the crafts. Craftsmen, as members of the American cultural and intellectual community, were coming into their own.

World War II disrupted all aspects of Western culture, including the crafts movement. The European craft community was scattered during the war, and America became the new home of many of the best European craftsmen. Sophisticated, mobile, refined, and educated, the European craftsmen brought with them the whole history of their own traditions as well as great insights into the arts of non-Western cultures, especially those of the Orient. American craftsmen responded with zeal and experienced both the vigor of hybridization and the malaise of eclecticism in the process. Postwar American crafts became stylistically refined and technically expert largely through the input of experience, creativity, and professional commitment of the Europeans.

5

By mid-century the stage was set for the full flowering of American crafts. Art schools and universities were beginning to provide sound economic security for craftsmen. The ongoing influx of European talent gave the craft scene fresh ideas and energy. American technology was being harnessed to new aesthetic possibilities, and the booming American economy was providing a new affluence and leisure for a population that had at last turned its attention to patronizing artists.

Of all the factors shaping American crafts, however, none was more significant than the geographic dispersal of craftsmen themselves across the entire country. The craftsmen's traditional spirit of independence and preference for a nonurban life-style guaranteed that the American craft world would not be dominated by a single group located in a single urban center. The Black Mountain School in North Carolina achieved prominence through the efforts of weavers, Anni Albers and Trude Guermonprez. Alfred University, in western New York, established itself as a major ceramics center under potter Daniel Rhodes. In Michigan Richard Thomas formalized the metalsmithing program at Cranbrook that had been started earlier by Arthur Nevill Kirk. In Guerneville, California, during the same period, Franz and Marguerite Wildenhain established the influential Pond Farm Pottery. Since 1950 the American craft world has enjoyed a truly national identity that blends personal and regional views into a composite cultural whole.

The ongoing craft movement today includes two distinct groups of craftsmen who can be separated from each other on the basis of their history and their attitudes toward product production. One group is committed to the making of utilitarian objects fashioned after particular prototypes. These are what have generally been called "production craftsmen." Their counterparts, the nonproduction craftsmen, concern themselves with the making of unique craft objects for special situations. In 1970 author-collector Lee Nordness wrote the book entitled *Objects U.S.A.*, which was the first publication to focus exclusively on the work of America's nonproduction craftsmen. Nordness recognized the differences between production and nonproduction craftsmen and felt the need for a new term that would better recognize nonproduction craftsmen in the contemporary art world. He ultimately called them *object makers*, and the name stuck. Nordness's object makers created works that ranged from the satiric to the sensuous, and from the expressionistic to the purely ornamental. The forms and ideas in today's nonproduction crafts have proliferated to the point that they can no longer be described under one inclusive label.

6

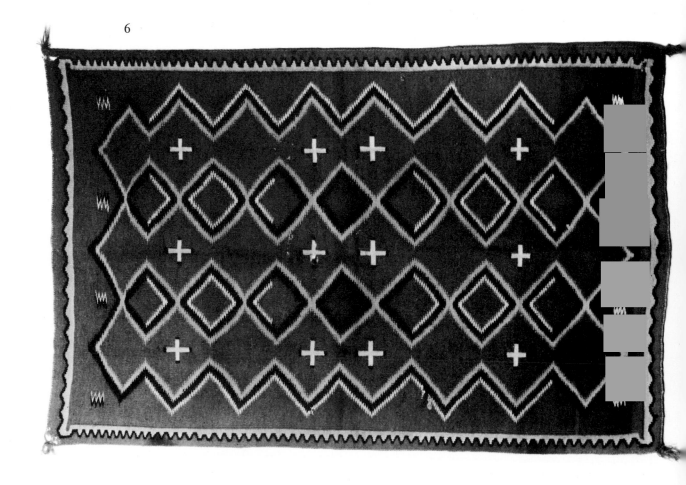

6. Navaho rug. c. 1880. Red, black, yellow, and white wool. 33″ x 50″. (Cranbrook Institute of Science, Bloomfield Hills, Michigan)

7. Eider duck decoy. Last quarter of nineteenth century. Polychromed wood. L. 14½″. Photograph by Thomas Wedell. (Author's collection)

7

The mainstream of nonproduction crafts has evolved out of the tradition of elegance. This tradition can be traced back into Western and Eastern crafts for centuries, but it assumed its present American form in the time of Louis Comfort Tiffany. This tradition is carried on by a centrist group of artists who have always been called *fine craftsmen*. Contemporary fine craftsmen work in a broad range of styles and materials but the objects they produce are always well designed, impeccably crafted, and imbued with an expression that is recognizably tied to a particular aesthetic.

Other modern nonproduction crafts have moved away from the fine-craft mainstream. Beginning with the Bauhaus, a group of craftsmen who could be labeled the *abstractionists* focused their work on pure composition and form. Intensely involved with the history of modern art, they have been highly influenced by movements from early Constructivism and Abstract Expressionism to present-day Op art and Minimal art. The *abstractionists* departed from considerations of function in favor of an emphasis on plastic issues and visual dynamics.

The Funk movement of the 1960s extended nonproduction crafts into another of its contemporary forms. Funk subtly blended Abstract Expressionism, Surrealism, and Dada with a native humor and an off-the-cuff vulgarity to produce an expression that both outraged and delighted Americans for a decade.

The bequest of Funk is seen today in the visions and fantasies of a new young generation that could be called the *imagists*. Combining whimsy with images from the world of dreams, these artists seek to charm and transport rather than to offend or provoke.

The concerns of other contemporary nonproduction craftsmen have been focused on spiritual and social issues. The *icon makers* create personal totems or eccentric fetishes for contemplation. Their work is inspired by the magic cult objects of primitive societies. The icon makers create highly personal statements rich in imagery to fill a void that they feel exists in the spiritual side of contemporary life.

A group that might best be called the *advocates* extends its creative energies into an exploration of art expressing some aspect of personal identity or social awareness. Their work touches issues of politics, ecology, ethnic identity, psychology, and the interaction of man and technology. The advocates speak out through their work to a public that they hope will heed their call to new social awakenings.

The last significant group of contemporary nonproduction craftsmen make large works for public spaces. The *monumentalists* of the last ten years are the direct heirs of the medieval tapestry makers and the Roman fountain builders. Both government and private industry have sought out these craftsmen to enrich the public environment in and around office buildings and commercial sites. Monumental fiber works and environmental clay or wood constructions have brought a new visual elegance and tactile richness to the centers of urban life.

At this point, these questions could be asked: What is the contemporary state of the production craft tradition? Has the traditional potter or woodworker become a casualty in our time? Surprisingly, in the face of much adversity, they persist. Outside of the spotlight of the new and the relevant, dedicated production craftsmen still make a living from their work. They make their living fiercely independent of the teaching system and undiscouraged by the caprice of art fashion. True to the vision of William Morris, they hold to the belief that disciplined hands shaping a good product, touched by the spark of creativity, can yield an important form of beauty to enrich the lives of people everywhere. The production craftsman in contemporary America still finds pride in an identity as a potter, or a weaver, or a woodworker. Production craftsmen live their identity and leave an indelible mark on American life.

This is a book about American crafts and craftsmen. The genealogies traced here are elaborated in the chapters that follow. The twenty-five years of work documented here speak well of the vigor that craftsmen have brought to their search, whether they are a part of the production crafts orthodoxy or the multifaceted nonproduction field. This is a book about the masters and innovators who have influenced American crafts. The crafts of a country are of the utmost importance because crafts reflect many aspects of a country's heritage and national character. In America today the crafts are exciting and varied. The material presented here provides a qualitative index to one aspect of America's art history, and, perhaps, offers insight into America's cultural future.

8

FOR USE AND BEAUTY

Glick

Karnes

Lyon

Maloof

McGlauchlin

Nakashima

Pearson

Rochester Folk Art Guild

Serkin

Shaner

Stocksdale

9. Conoid table. George K. Nakashima. 1965. English walnut. L. 80″. Photograph by Michael Hall.

The production or "use" craftsman is absolutely central to any definition of the crafts. Throughout history, production craftsmen have faced the challenge of producing functional ware to serve and grace man's life and they have created a craft tradition that is as rich and varied as the entire spectrum of human culture. Their history touches the Navaho weavers of New Mexico, the Jomon potters of Japan, and the glass molders of the Etruscan civilization. The production lineage has provided some of the world's most profound artworks.

The fact that the sometimes anonymous and always unselfconscious production craftsman has followed a different path from the "fine" craftsman has resulted in a tradition with an aesthetic all its own. The work from this tradition is understated rather than luxurious, informal rather than formal, and simple rather than ornamental. It is never overloaded with superfluous detail. It never appears overly intellectual or overly fastidious. Work from the use tradition has a dignity and restraint that comes from honest service. The best use crafts have always reflected a perfect balance between the useful and the beautiful.

Despite their illustrious history, true production craftsmen make up only a small part of the modern craft world. Today's use craftsmen have survived against the threat of assimilation or outright extinction that has faced them since the middle of the nineteenth century. This threat is rooted in simple economics. In the twentieth century efficient machines cheaply produce most of the things that traditionally were made by the craftsman's hand. Ironically the affluence born of technology and mechanization may yet hold the key to the survival of the production craftsman. The American consumer, after half a century of fascination with the products of machines, has finally begun to desire handmade goods. This demand has lifted production crafts out of competition with machine-made products. The new use craftsman asks us to consider the "quality of life" as something quite different from the "necessities of living." The production potter offers us the beauty of a salt-glazed jar as an alternative to the plastic dishes that set most tables. The production weaver gives us the richness of handwoven fabrics over the sterile prints produced bolt after bolt by the textile industry. Although continued by a relatively small number of craftsmen, the use tradition in America has remained visible and viable. Each generation spawns its masters and the energy of this tradition perseveres with unwavering character and dignity.

10

11

12. *Landscape Slab*. David Shaner. 1972. Stoneware. 12" x 14". (Artist's collection)

13. Teapot. David Shaner. 1970. Salt-glazed stoneware. H. 10"; W. 6". (Artist's collection)

14. Decorative bowl. Bob Stocksdale. 1976. Cambodian boxwood. H. 4½"; W. 9". (Philadelphia Museum of Art)

12

13

As a designer, the use craftsman strives for beauty that is nonacademic, unaffected, and comfortably evolved from functional requirements. The crafts from the production tradition are made to be used. Their forms evolve from the belief that "form follows function." Bedspreads and rugs must hold their shape and color; pitchers must be lightweight and pour correctly; chairs must be sturdy; and metal flatware and containers serviceable and easily cleaned. The beauty from the production tradition is not derived from lofty treatises on aesthetics but is based, instead, on natural laws of proportion and balance. The best production crafts can be understood and appreciated by anyone with eyes and hands and the time to touch and see.

Sam Maloof has been making furniture for over twenty years. His work is functional, honest, and untouched by fussy detail. Maloof's production is steady and impressive. His output of completed furniture items and accessories numbers in the thousands. Two or three times a year Maloof introduces a prototype for a new piece. Once a prototype is perfected, Maloof will work from it indefinitely because he believes that trends and fashion are transient, but classic design and good craftsmanship will endure over time.

Maloof's widely known cradles are fine examples of the production craftsman's art. They have uniqueness of design, obvious serviceability, and integrity of form. Maloof is totally committed to the tradition of production crafts in

14

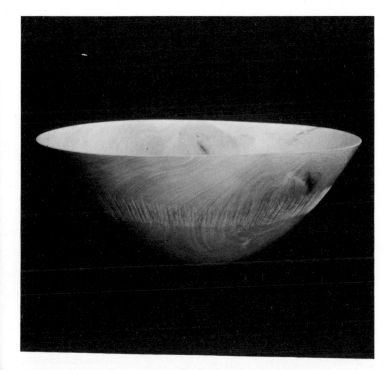

America. He serves as a trustee for the American Crafts Council, a position from which he hopes to help young craftsmen become independent and contributing members of society.

Many of America's production craftsmen exhibit a decided preference for rural life. They purposely establish their studios in secluded, and often out-of-the-way places. They enjoy the land and nature. They are more interested in working in solitude than in promoting their work. Montana's David Shaner, in a letter to the author, wrote, ". . . I make my living potting [since 1963] . . . I chose to live in a beautiful remote area of the country—if all of this affects my work, it is OK by me." Shaner's pots evoke the sense of the bold, bleak Montana landscape where they are made, as much as the earthiness of the clay from which they are formed. Pots, potter, and potting—for Shaner they are one and inseparable.

Potter Karen Karnes has spent many years dedicated to the making of durable stoneware vessels in her studio in Stony Point, New York. Although she has done a few special commissions, the majority of her time is committed to making utilitarian ware. Her production is centered around several types of storage vessels, all of which have a distinctive, full, inviting form. Her jars seem to echo the rocks and streams of the upstate New York landscape. Her slips of orange and blue are synchronized with the dappled grays and tans of the natural clay. Dignified and quiet, this pottery reflects the intense yet simple life of the production potter.

15

15. Jar. Karen Karnes. 1976. Salt-glazed stoneware. H. 13″; W. 9″. Photograph by Lucy Massie Phenix.

16. Vase. Karen Karnes. 1975. Salt-glazed stoneware. H. 14″; W. 12″. Photograph by Lucy Massie Phenix.

17. Covered jar. Karen Karnes. 1976. Salt-glazed stoneware. H. 10″; W. 12″. Photograph by Lucy Massie Phenix.

16

17

18

18. Fireset. Rochester Folk Art Guild. 1976. Iron fireset with upset handles. L. 32″.

19. Letter opener. Ronald Hayes Pearson. 1975. Sterling silver. L. 9″. Photograph by Bob Hanson.

20. Bracelets. Ronald Hayes Pearson. 1975. Sterling silver. W. 1″; W. ⅜″; W. 2″. Photograph by Bob Hanson.

19

Karnes's calendar revolves around an orderly sequence of clay mixing, throwing, trimming, and firing. This work cycle rises to a crescendo during the firing of the ware. At white heat, rock salt is thrown into the fiery kiln chamber where it volatilizes, coating each pot with a glossy pebble finish that is the Karnes trademark. After the cooling and the unstacking of the kiln, the cycle begins anew as fresh clay is mixed and thrown.

Karnes's approach to the art of pottery making varies little from that of the ancients. Her studio is simple. Her tools are basic, and the processes she uses bypass most of the complex technology potentially available to her. Like all production craftsmen, Karnes does not believe that tedious techniques or elaborate procedures are integral to the creation of strong work. Marked by directness and refined to an honest simplicity, Karnes's vessels epitomize the aspirations of the production craftsmen working in the United States today.

Woodworker Robert Stocksdale turns a variety of bowls and plates in his basement studio in Berkeley, California. He divides his time between the studio and a wide-ranging search for the rare and exotic woods that he favors for his production. Surrounded by an orderly arrangement of turning tools and the pungent odor of curing wood, Stocksdale is at home working and living a rhythm that is in constant harmony with the hum of his lathe.

Production craftsmen arrive at an art statement through a process that is directly linked to production itself. For them, time spent in duplication or slow modification of a form is never simply an exercise of manual skills. It is rather a focus of artistic activity leading directly to expanded creative realizations. There is a universal understanding among

20

22

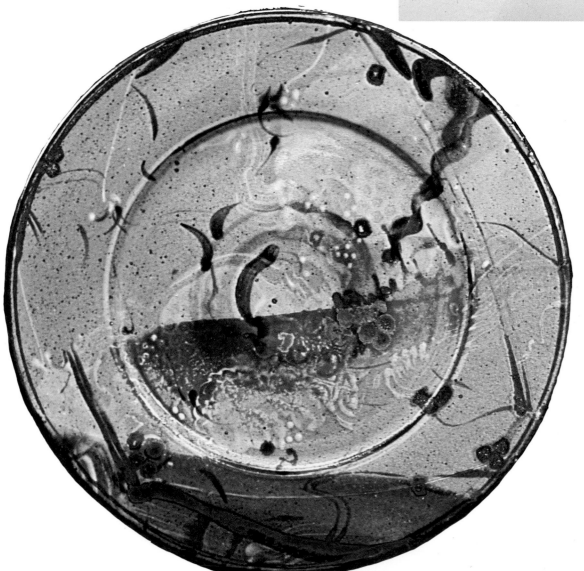

21

21. Platter. John Glick. 1976. Reduction-fired stoneware. Diam. 18″. Photograph by Robert Vigiletti.

22. Steam bubble vase. Tom McGlauchlin. 1973. Hand-blown dichroic glass. H. 9″. Photograph by Tom McGlauchlin.

23. Hand-blown glass vase. Tom McGlauchlin. 1975. Opalescent glass. H. 8½″. Photograph by Tom McGlauchlin.

23

use craftsmen that the production approach to art has an expressive potential that transcends mere repetition. When asked how he could repeat the same brush design on his pots for thirty years, Japan's great potter, Shoji Hamada, replied that he felt that the designs were never the same twice. "Even if I tried to repeat, the pigment, brush, my arm, and the thought would be different" (Bernard Leach, *The Potter's Challenge*, New York: E. P. Dutton, 1975). This seemingly romantic philosophy is consummately realistic and has given the world some of its greatest art objects. Today's American use craftsmen join Hamada in the belief that great production crafts result from a mysterious alchemy blending the mind, the hand, and the intuition to transform inert materials into timeless art.

Glass artist Tom McGlauchlin's rhythmic swings of the blowpipe are as practiced and graceful as any dance. Continually perfecting several basic forms, McGlauchlin slowly brings out the fluid potential of his glass. Each intense session with the form and the fire yields more knowledge of form and an evolution of artistic ideas. Although McGlauchlin works with only a few basic shapes, no two pieces of his work are exactly alike. Using different coloring oxides and different patterns of trailings on his surfaces, he endlessly varies his vases, plates, and bottles. McGlauchlin's colors

24. Box. John Glick. 1976. Reduction-fired stoneware. L. 7". Photograph by Robert Vigiletti.

25. Decanter with wine goblets and tumblers. Rochester Folk Art Guild. 1976. Glass with pulled appliqué decoration. H. of decanter: 9".

24

range from transparent off-pinks and Art Nouveau greens to milky blues and oranges. All of these colors are swirled into his prodigious output of glassware, which is as serviceable as it is handsome.

The time of production and the cost of precious metals have drastically reduced the number of metalworkers who will accept the hardships of production smithing. Maine's Ronald Pearson has continued to work on forms in series despite the pressure to make one-of-a-kind pieces. Although he does make unique works, he is consistently committed to certain forms in metal that can be produced in numbers without losing their character or strength. His expert forging brings out the ductile qualities of the metal, giving his bracelets a soft, sensuous, and understated look. His letter opener is as simple and graceful as Constantin Brancusi's *Bird in Flight*. Pearson works with many metals, giving his distinctive touch to every piece that comes from his studio.

The training of early American craftsmen was accomplished through a rigid apprenticeship system that encouraged the transmission of techniques and styles from master to apprentice. Apprentices learned their craft skills through meticulous practice of all steps of a trade, from menial chores to the creative act itself. Today's art schools and universities sometimes tend to overlook the value of this discipline in favor of a more experimental approach to the search for style and personal expression. Production craftsmen still value apprenticeship as a way of learning and they enjoy passing their knowledge on to younger people through practical working situations in studios rather than in classrooms.

25

26

26. Conoid bench with back.
George K. Nakashima. 1962.
English walnut with hickory
spindles. L. 84″. Photograph
courtesy Time-Life, Inc.

27. *Mountain Landscape*.
Pillow. Nancy Lyon. Pro-
duction piece. Weaving (wool
warp technique with all
handspun wool weft, inlay
technique on block weave).
16″ x 16″.

28. Poncho. Lucy J. Serkin.
1975. Wool. 54″ x 72″.
Photograph by John Serkin.

Although he has an endless list of waiting apprentices, furniture maker George Nakashima is very particular about the people who work in his shop. He prefers local helpers to the legions of art or architecture students who seek part-time work in his studio. He feels that transient apprentices rarely have the patience truly to learn his craft. The average stay for a member of his staff is ten to fifteen years, far longer than a break between semesters.

Nakashima has lived and worked in New Hope, Pennsylvania, for thirty-two years. Over the years he has built an extensive complex of studios, showrooms, storage sheds, and dwellings. Here he makes his fine furniture for use and beauty. Using woods from England, France, and from the "trees of the great forests where Iran, Turkey, and Russia meet," Nakashima crafts a distinctive line of tables, cabinets, and benches. He also uses large planks of American cherry and walnut. As his choice of woods is a blend of the native and the exotic, so, too, his art is a personal blend that celebrates early American country furniture, Japanese architecture, and contemporary Scandinavian design. Each piece of Nakashima furniture is a unique aesthetic synthesis in which the artist's ideas are intertwined with the natural idiosyncrasies and burls of the wood. Nakashima is so particular about his work that he travels hundreds of miles from his studio to supervise personally the first major cutting of the logs he has selected. He directs each cut as the trees pass through the gigantic saws of the mill, specifying exactly which aspect of the grain should be exposed in the final planks. In this way he can make aesthetic decisions at an early point in order to control his work from its inception to its final coatings of lemon oil.

Nakashima sees himself as a determined survivor of better times, an anachronism in contemporary society. His determination to give America fine craftsmanship and aesthetic integrity should serve as an example to young craftsmen just beginning their careers. His deep feeling for his work and for his material is beautifully stated in this paragraph from his privately printed studio catalogue:

A tree is perhaps our most intimate contact with nature— A tree sits like an avatar, immutable, beyond the pains of man—There are even specimens like the Yakusugi, which in a single life has spanned the entire history of civilized man as we know him—Hundreds of generations of men have marched past—Civilizations much greater than ours have risen and have gone to dust . . . We have the audacity to work this material—In a sense it is our Yoga, our union with the Divine.

Expression, in the artistic sense, flows from the production craftsman's subconscious through the act of working. Bernard Leach, talking of potters in *A Potters Book* (1967), speaks for all production craftsmen when he says:

He is faced with a broken tradition, and what is even more serious, with a culture in rapid process of change . . . Only the artist and craftsman of unusual perception and strength of character stands a chance of selecting what is best from the welter of ideas which rolls in upon him today . . . Sincerity is what matters, and according to the degree in which the vital force of the potter and that of his culture behind him flow through the process of making, the resulting pot will have life in it or not.

There is unquestionably something simple and consistently autobiographical registered in all things born of honest production. Although honesty is important, today's use craftsman knows that honesty is only half of the battle. It also takes time, work, and vision to give work the same qualities that put any of the great craft objects of history in our memories forever. From the hands of the masters flow the subtle mysterious sensibilities that mark the production craft masterpieces that are plucked from common service to be preserved as art treasures in museums around the world.

33

34

35

36

37

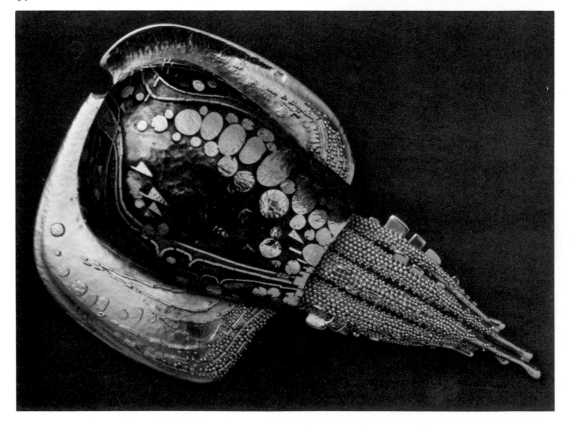

36. *Cephalopod Series.*
Pendant brooch. John Paul
Miller. 1975. Constructed
from 18 k. gold and enamel.

37. *Cephalopod Series.*
Pendant brooch. John Paul
Miller. 1972. Constructed
from 18 k. gold and enamel.

38. Untitled. Choker
neckpiece. Eleanor Moty.
1972. Photo-etched and
electroformed silver with
quartz crystals and acrylic.
7″ x 2″. Photograph by
Eleanor Moty.

39. Choker. Margret Craver.
1976. 22 k. gold wire, *en
résille* enamel. (Josephine
Withers)

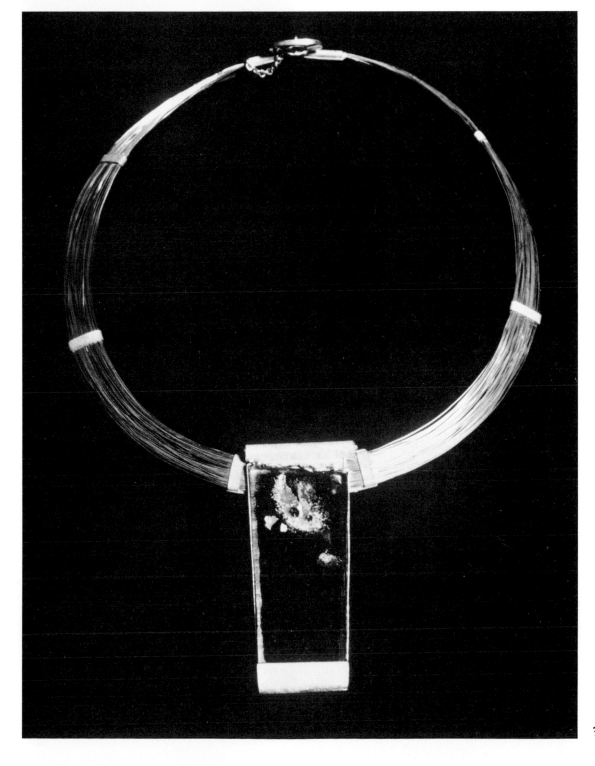

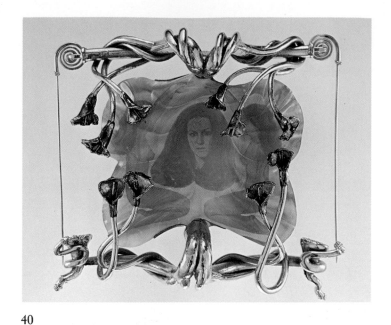

40

40. *Cameo Brooch*. Stanley Lechtzin. 1973. Cast polyester photo image with electroformed silver gilt. 6" x 6½" x 2".

41. *Torque*. Stanley Lechtzin. 1972. Cast opalized polyester and electroformed silver gilt. 7½" x 15" x 2".

Fine crafts are typified by their refinement of appearance. This refinement is a mirror of the fine craftsman's own aesthetic sensibility. This sensibility can best be called *decorative*, but this term requires some clarification before it can be appropriately set into any discussion of the fine crafts today.

Contemporary art criticism has cast the notion of the decorative in an increasingly negative light. The modern "less is more" aesthetic in the fine arts suggests that almost anything not purely structural is of necessity superfluous or frivolous. The crafts have felt the onslaught of this critical bias, and craftsmen of the 1950s were sharply divided over this issue. The purists branded anything technically accomplished as too "slick." The decorative, however, has always had its place in art. In the broadest sense, early man decorated his living environment with the paintings on the walls of his cave dwellings. The decorative dimension in such art as Egyptian frescoes or Byzantine mosaics cannot be denied. Today these facts are being reappraised, and the critical pendulum has swung back to a place where many craftsmen are proud of the decorative quality of their work. The word *decorative* once again is used to describe properly one artistic element that runs deeply through many aspects of visual culture.

Since the Arts and Crafts Revival of the last century, a highly sophisticated sense of materials has surrounded the fine crafts. Haunting museums and libraries, several generations of craftsmen have discovered a rich treasure trove of ideas and inspirations from the wood, fiber, and ceramic works of other cultures. A glance through the illustrations in this chapter will reveal the numerous sources for the complex styles of today's fine crafts. Medieval goldwork and weaponry from northern Europe have left their marks on contemporary jewelry. Feathered capes and delicate weavings discovered in Peruvian mummy bundles have influenced both the technique and design of much modern textile work. The American Indian's sensitive use of fur and feathers in

42

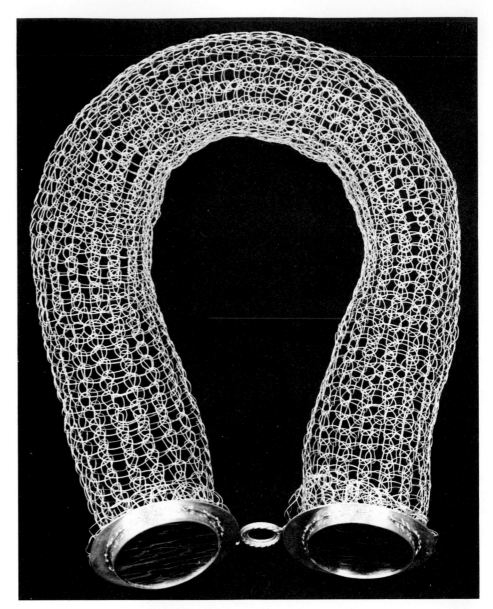

43

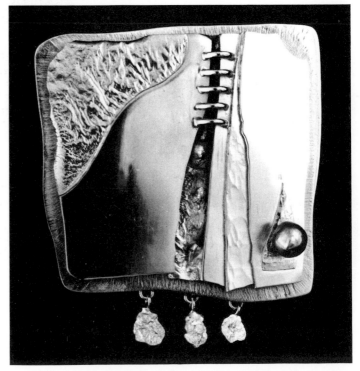

44

29

30

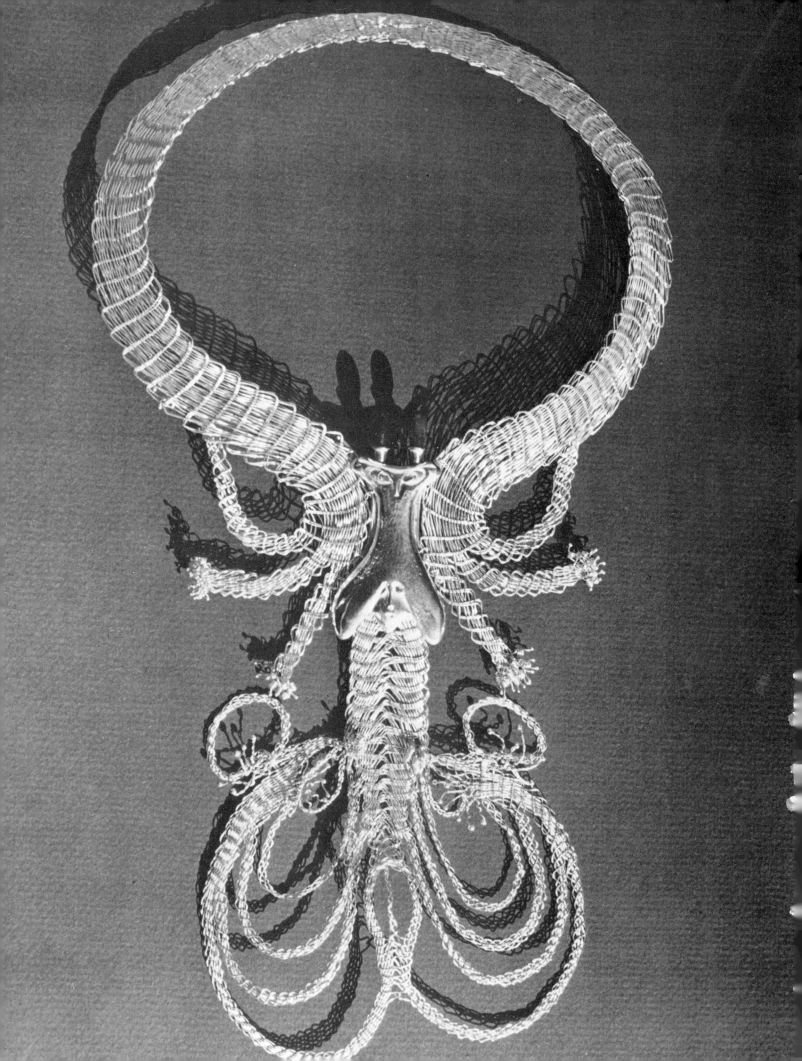

THE TRADITION OF ELEGANCE

Al-Hilali
Carpenter
Castle
Chihuly
Craver
Dailey
Ebendorf
Erickson
Esherick
Evans
Fisch
Grotell
Guermonprez

Higby
Hu
Kaufman
Kosheleff
Labino
Lechtzin
Lipke
Lloyd
Miller
Moty
Noffke
Samuels
Skoogfors
Soldner
Stephenson
Strong
Woell
Woodman

31. Necklace with pendant.
Arline M. Fisch. 1975.
Braided fine silver, clasp
chased sterling. L. 12".
Photograph by Michael Hall.

32. Bird. Mary Lee Hu.
1969. Fine silver, garnets. H.
4½″. Photograph by Mary
Lee Hu.

33. *Cephalopod Series.*
Pendant brooch. John Paul
Miller. 1970. Constructed
from 18 k. gold and enamel.

34. Pin. Bob Ebendorf.
1975. Gold-plated silver,
pearls, and plexiglass. H. 3″.
Photograph by Evon
Streetman.

35. *Feather Lady.* Brooch.
Arline M. Fisch. 1971.
Fire-gilt chased sterling silver,
plastic resin, and parrot
feathers. 5″ x 5″. Photograph
by Michael Hall.

The majority of working craftsmen in America today can be labeled "fine craftsmen." Historically, the fine craftsman made chalices for the church rather than iron door latches for the ordinary home. The blacksmith in the streets always had a goldsmith counterpart in the service of the court. It is from this goldsmith that the contemporary fine craftsman has inherited the tradition of elegance.

The tradition of elegance is a history of unique objects created for an elite patronage. Fine crafts have found their use in particular formal ceremonies and circumstances. Fine craftsmen have always produced work meant to be appreciated aesthetically first and functionally second. This view has lent an inherent formality to the tradition itself.

The fine craftsman's creative consciousness is balanced between the active and the contemplative aspects of the artistic process. Fine craftsmen work at a pace that allows them ample time for the careful execution of details. The orientation of the fine craftsman also includes a process of evaluation that measures each newly completed work against the artist's stated aesthetic goals. It is precisely this formality of approach to creative endeavor that separates the fine craftsman from the more unselfconscious and intuitive production craftsman.

32

the embellishment of apparel and religious paraphernalia has inspired fine craftsmen in many areas to incorporate these fragile materials in their work. The jurors' statement, from a 1974 exhibition entitled "The Goldsmith" at the Renwick Gallery, Smithsonian Institution, acknowledged the new explorations of materials generated, in part, by contemporary appreciations of the art of other cultures. Commenting on recent trends in jewelry and metalwork, the jurors said: "There is a noticeable interest in the mixing of metals, in the use of plastics, in the inclusion of nonprecious and nonpermanent materials such as fiber, feathers, and leather." Today's fine craftsman is a creative eclectic, finding new and highly personal applications for techniques and materials found in the works of other hands in other places and times.

A look at the tradition of elegance in America begins in the field of metalwork. Always respected, the classic jeweler and metalsmith have carried the history of fine crafts across political boundaries and across time. Whether working on commissions or developing work independently for sale in shops and galleries, today's metal craftsmen are, in many ways, the primary inheritors of the tradition of elegance.

42. *Great American Themes: The Only Good Indian Is a Dead Indian*. Pendant. J. Fred Woell. Brass, silver, copper. H. 2¾″; W. 2½″; D. ¼″. Photograph by J. Fred Woell.

43. *Knitted Necklace*. Arline M. Fisch. 1974. Spool-knitted fine silver, sterling silver, azure antique glass. Diam. of tube: 2″.

44. Pin. Olaf Skoogfors. 1973. Reticulated sections of gold-plated sterling silver with blue baroque pearl. H. 2½″; W. 2¼″. Photograph by Olaf Skoogfors.

45. *Nip Grain Goblet*. Gary Noffke. 1973. Silver chased and stamped with 18 k. gold appliqué. Seamed raising. H. 5″; maximum Diam. 2½″. (Artist's collection)

45

46

46. Drum. Jan Brooks Lloyd. 1973. Brass, steel, leather, goatskin, resins, padauk wood sticks. H. approx. 10″.

47. Carved desk. Wharton Esherick. 1927. Red oak. H. 79″. Photograph courtesy The Brooklyn Museum. (The Wharton Esherick Museum, Paoli, Pennsylvania)

48. Three chairs (from a set of four). Wharton Esherick. 1928. Walnut with ebony strips. Photograph courtesy The Brooklyn Museum. (Peter Esherick)

Margret Craver was one of the first modern American metalworkers. She traveled to Europe to study under master goldsmiths during the late 1930s, and then returned home to revive the art of metalworking in her own country. Independently, she has researched the difficult sixteenth-century French technique of *en résille* enameling. Her elegant pins and brooches are touched by a simplicity of form and a richness of surface that shaped an entire aesthetic in the field of jewelry.

Goldsmith John Paul Miller has also redefined and extended the tradition of elegance. Inspired by exotic forms of sea life, Miller creates jewelry that is distinctive in appearance and impeccable in workmanship. His precise pendants juxtapose the smooth forms and sinuous textured shapes of tiny squid and ephemeral corals. The delicate textures incorporated in Miller's work are achieved by means of a very ancient process called *granulation,* which the artist researched and adapted to his own needs. Very much a contemporary jeweler, John Paul Miller still captures the timelessness of nature in his work. Miller links the history of metalworking to a personal expression of his own feelings about the mysterious sources of life itself.

California metalsmith Arline Fisch shapes her art from sources that reach deep into the past of many cultures. Talking about her point of view, she said, in an interview with the author, "My work comes from older historical things. I look at contemporary things but I don't feed off of them." Her work is touched by Egyptian, Incan, and even barbarian motifs from Northern Europe. The integration of these varying motifs into very wearable forms of jewelry becomes particularized through Fisch's personal sensitivity to materials ranging from gold to parrot feathers. An ongoing involvement with woven metal necklaces and bracelets has extended Fisch's personal artistic expression and reinforces the viable relationship between tradition and invention in the fine craftsman's search for new images.

47

48

49. Harp guitar, two balalaikas. Francis M. Kosheleff. 1975. Harp guitar: spruce, various African woods; balalaikas: rosewood and walnut. Harp size of classical guitar. Photograph by Jim Dixon.

50. Game table and chairs. Arthur Carpenter. 1970. Walnut, rosewood, and cherry. 33″ x 33″. Photograph by Arthur Carpenter.

51. *Three-seat Laminated Couch.* Wendell Castle. 1968. Laminated cherry. H. 32″; W. 84″; D. 36″. Photograph by Bruce Miller. (Artist's collection)

52. Rocking chair. Wendell Castle. 1975. Zebrawood and suede leather. H. 36″; W. 28″; D. 36″. Photograph by Bruce Miller.

51

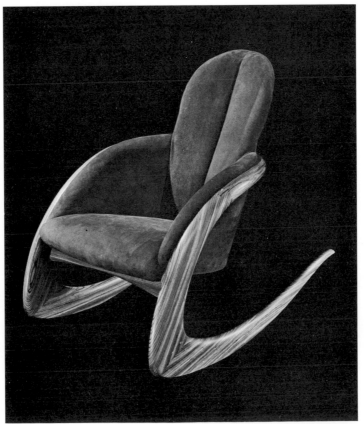

52

53

In Philadelphia, artist Stanley Lechtzin has moved the jeweler's art into phase with contemporary advances in metal- and plastic-forming technology. Lechtzin works in a unique studio where he has built an entire electroforming laboratory. He fashions metal shapes for his jewelry by a process that is his own adaptation of modern industrial electroforming techniques. His metal shapes are often attached to powerful horn-like polyester configurations to form exciting necklaces and other pieces of fine jewelry. Like Louis Tiffany, three-quarters of a century earlier, Stanley Lechtzin has harnessed the technology around him in the service of his own creative vision.

Fine woodworking in America, like fine metalworking, developed from a few determined innovators who found their education through aggressive search and experimentation. Pennsylvania woodworker, Wharton Esherick (1887–1970) almost single-handedly established the twentieth-century style of American woodworking. Possessing the eye of a sculptor, the hands of a master cabinetmaker, and a very particular inspiration, Esherick pushed the limits of wood as a fine craft medium until the very end of his long and productive life. His studio-home near Philadelphia remains one of the most celebrated craft monuments of the century. Esherick's unique executions of the wood details in this building, from the furniture to the walls and staircase, have profoundly influenced almost all contemporary woodcraftsmen working today.

In the 1960s Wendell Castle opened the Esherick vocabulary to new possibilities with his fresh ideas in free-formed sculptured furniture. In his studio in Rochester, New York, Castle began to develop visceral flowing organic furniture constructed from laminated wood. This work gained quick recognition for its unique design and highly tactile utilization of the richness of hand-finished wood.

Castle's complete knowledge of good design is felt in every aspect of his furniture. His chairs and couches are shaped to conform to fitted cloth seats and bolsters made to his specifications and covered in bright fabrics. His cabinets have individually shaped drawers that nestle perfectly in their allotted spaces, opening to the lightest touch.

53. Miscellaneous examples of furniture. Arthur Carpenter. 1971. Wood. Photograph by Arthur Carpenter.

54. Scallop-shell desk with wishbone chair. Arthur Carpenter. 1975. Walnut and lacewood. H. 36″; W. 36″; D. 20″. Photograph by Michael Hall.

55. (Overleaf, page 56). Jar. Paul Soldner. 1974. Raku-fired ceramic. H. 10½″. Photograph by Michael Hall.

56. (Overleaf, page 57). *Serape Style, 1865*. Glass cylinder (Navaho Blanket series). Dale Chihuly. 1975. Blown glass. H. 8″. Photograph by Allan Thelin. (Peter Voulkos)

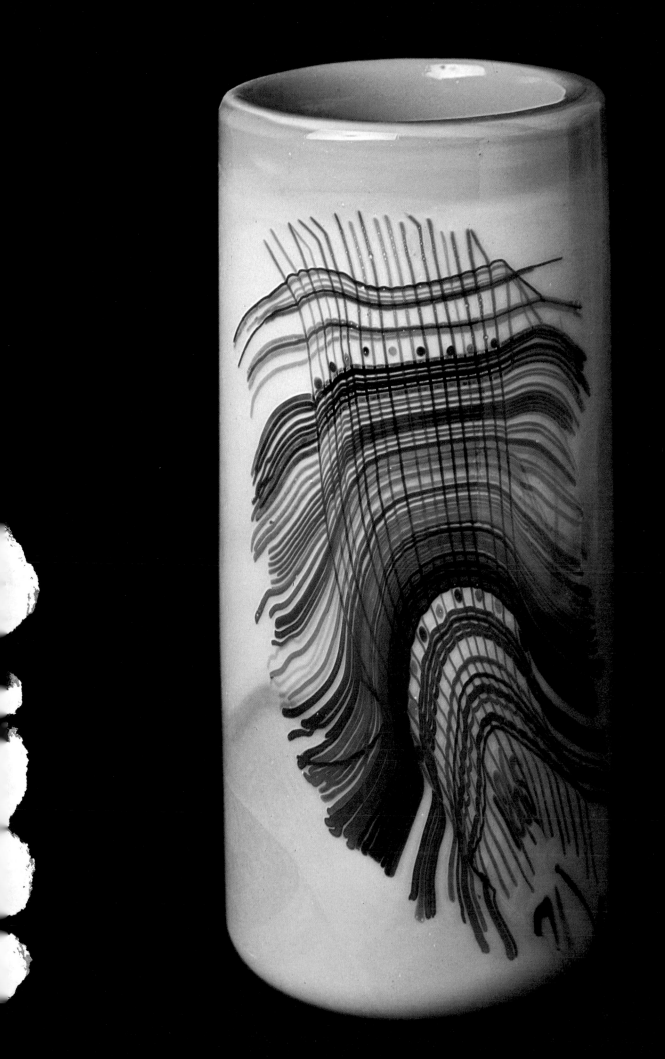

57

58

58

57. Chalice. Dominick Labino. 1973. Multicolored festooning on opaque white glass cased in colorless glass. H. 6¾". Photograph by Ray Bossert. (Artist's collection)

58. *Spring Things.* Blown form. Dominick Labino. 1974. Hot-tooled design encased in colorless glass. H. 8½". Photograph by Ray Bossert. (Artist's collection)

59. *Lasso Cups.* Randy Strong. 1973. Blown glass. H. 6". Photograph by Randy Strong. (Artist's collection)

Over the past few years, Castle has extended his explorations of furniture ideas into the medium of plastic. His fiberglass furniture has evolved as another extension of a very personal sculptural vocabulary. In both wood and plastic, Wendell Castle has produced significant work that has found its way into the homes of discriminating craft patrons.

Arthur Carpenter of Bolinas, California, is another contemporary woodworker whose oeuvre has added scope to the tradition of elegance. Carpenter, known professionally as Espenet, stresses function and design in his work. His furniture is carefully and beautifully constructed to take maximum advantage of the rich grain patterns in wood. Espenet frequently works several woods together into a single form, using light-colored woods to give linear accents to dark walnut shapes. Espenet's studio has become a mecca for young woodworkers seeking contact with the contemporary fine craft mainstream. In Arthur Carpenter they find a stringent teacher who demands excellence in the production of fine furniture of classic proportion and dignity.

59

60. *Abstract Geometric Motif*. Vase. Dan Dailey. 1976. Selenium glass with sandblasted pattern. H. 10″. Photograph by S. J. Cushner. (Artist's collection)

61. *Saddle Blanket*. Glass cylinder. Dale Chihuly. 1975. Blown glass. H. 10″. Photograph by Morgan Rockhill. (Mrs. Malcolm Grear)

62. Vase. Maija Grotell. 1942. Ceramic. H. 7¾″. Photograph by Thomas Wedell. (Sylvia Swanson)

63

The American fine glass revival came later than the revival of fine woodworking. The glass movement was launched dramatically in 1962 at a historic workshop held at The Toledo Museum of Art in Ohio. The workshop catalyzed a commitment to glass for ceramist Harvey Littleton who had been invited to direct the project. The technical problems at the workshop were met and eventually solved by a consulting industrial glass expert named Dominick Labino. Labino and Littleton emerged from the Toledo workshop as the fathers of today's glass movement. In the years following the seminar, they both traveled across the country helping to establish glass workshops everywhere and encouraging American glassblowers to take their place in the fine craft tradition.

In a studio laboratory outside Toledo, Labino has attempted to unlock the technical and chemical secrets of the ancient glassworkers. He has had great success in this effort, particularly in rediscovering the sand-casting methods used by the Etruscans to create the exquisite small glass bottles that are one of the hallmarks of their civilization. Labino's own work blends his historical perspective and technical expertise into an elegant contemporary glass expression that brings enrichment to living spaces all across America.

Dale Chihuly is the epitome of the sophisticated glass artist. He has explored his medium as a studio glassblower and as a master designer for both Steuben Glass in New York and the Vennini Fàbbrica of Venice. Chihuly has mastered all techniques of working both hot and cold glass and has even experimented with neon tubing and other forms of commercial glass. His artistic concepts move fluently through the complete range of glass expressions both historic and contemporary.

64

65

66

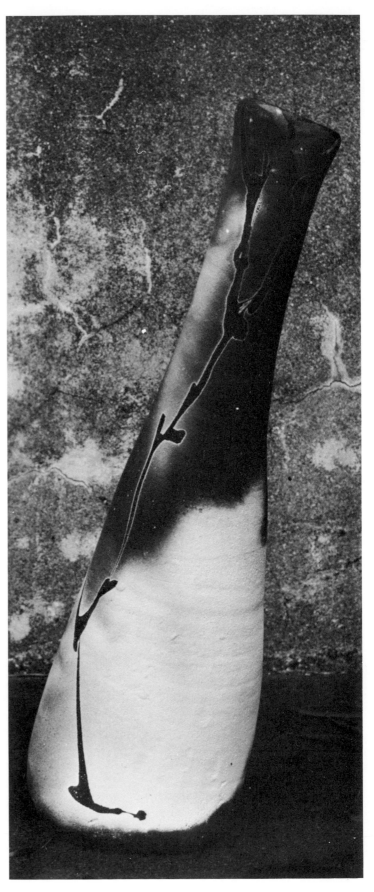

67

66. Jar. Paul Soldner. 1974.
Raku-fired ceramic.
H. approx. 22".

67. Vase. Paul Soldner.
1974. Raku-fired ceramic.
H. approx. 17".

Chihuly's recent magnificent cylinder series blends the natural primitive elegance of American Indian design with the technically and aesthetically cognizant art of the modern craftsman. The designs for the cylinders are begun as sketches, which are then translated into patterns of small, colored glass rods. Red-hot blown-glass cylinders are then rolled across the rods fusing the patterns onto the cylinders' surfaces. The Indian-inspired motifs are purposefully distorted during this process and emerge as wavy elusive imprints across the surfaces of the finished forms. The mastery and refinement of this work are seen in the artist's deft integration of strong primary colors and gentle pastels into a personal expression unique to the several traditions from which it evolves.

Chihuly divides his energy between lecturing, teaching, working in his studio, and exhibiting his work around the world. Totally committed to the magic of his medium, Dale Chihuly has rediscovered the beauty of the glass of yesterday and is creating new beauty in the glass of tomorrow.

The younger generation of glassworkers has extended the medium in new directions. California glass artist Jim Erickson works in forms that evolve from the tradition of stained glass. His hand-set glass windows orchestrate natural light and the luminescence of man-made glass into forms and images that boldly update Tiffany's work of three-quarters of a century ago.

In the history of modern American crafts, the classic ceramics tradition was shaped largely by a generation of European potters who immigrated here in the early part of this century. Finnish-born Maija Grotell (1899–1973) influenced the American fine craft view through the clay work that she created at Cranbrook from the 1930s through the 1950s. Grotell's austere container forms were embellished with bold deco patterns and often accented with brilliant gold or silver luster glazes. Her artistic insistence that each of her pots have its own unique identity set a precedent that has been followed by many American ceramists up to the present.

68. *Firewall Canyon.* Plate. Wayne Higby. 1975. Earthenware. 9½" x 9½".

69. *Oblique Angles #2.* Wall hanging. Riet Samuels. 1972. Double-cloth wool. 30" x 17½".

70. Jar. Susan G. Stephenson. 1975. Porcelain with low-fire luster-glaze. H. 10½".

71. Plant stand. Betty Woodman. 1974. Salt-fired porcelain. H. 27". Photograph by George Woodman. (Duncan Pollock)

Potter Paul Soldner is one of the most important fine craftsmen working in clay today. Soldner is best known for his large vase forms that are boldly decorated with calligraphic splashes of glaze cutting across their raw, smoke-blackened surfaces. Fascinated by old Japanese raku pots, Soldner revived the raku process and adapted it in a most personal way to his own style. Soldner's pots and platters stand unchallenged as unique creative statements and as brilliant syntheses of the old and the new in the potters' craft.

Soldner has also left his mark as a teacher. From the clay studios at Scripps College in Claremont, California, he has encouraged an entire generation of younger potters to experiment with building their own kilns and developing new approaches to clay as an artistic medium. Soldner also travels widely, offering pottery-making demonstrations and "kiln building" workshops that have kept new ideas moving through the American clay world. He has rounded out his busy schedule with the design and manufacture of potter's wheels and clay mixers uniquely suited to the needs and expectations of today's clay artists.

Alfred University potter Wayne Higby is representative of the newest group of American ceramists who have become a vital part of the tradition of elegance. Higby molds large covered jars that he embellishes with appliqué strips of clay that depict landscape scenes. Visually, the images of the landscapes emerge and then recede, as the colors and patterns suggest perceptions alternately referential and abstract, flat and three-dimensional. Although Higby's plates and jars can be used, their beauty and their delicacy make them works to be appreciated for visual rather than func-

70

71

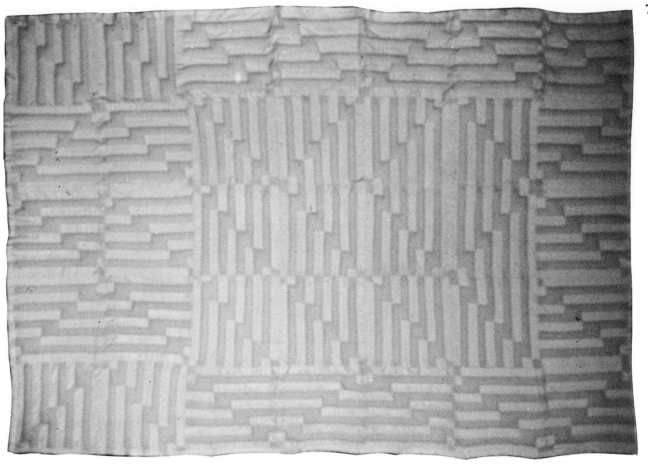

72. Untitled. Black and white reversible quilt. Deborah Kaufman. 1974. Canvas, satin, and taffeta fibers. 56″ x 78″. Photograph by Deborah Kaufman.

73. *Hand Quilt*. Deborah Kaufman. 1974. Corduroy and silk fibers from old ties. 75″ x 90″. Photograph by Deborah Kaufman.

74. *Puffed-up Mountain/Clouds*. Wall hanging. Kathryn McCardle Lipke. 1972. Silk screen printed, quilted, and stuffed. H. 60″; W. 100″; D. 6″. Photograph by Kathryn McCardle Lipke. (Private collection)

tional qualities. Wayne Higby is a fine craftsman who joins a landscape painter's vision to a plastic expression unique to the medium of clay.

Fiber, like clay, has a long history as a fine craft medium in America. The California weaver Trude Guermonprez (1910–1976) epitomized the classic tradition in her field. As both an artist and a highly influential teacher, Guermonprez left her mark on the fiber world. Her tapestry landscapes and portraits were always crafted with classical precision, and yet they pulsed with a veiled sense of mystery and atmosphere. In Guermonprez's work each woven image seems to be a window to an earth-tone world of shapes and symbols. Using the built-in structural geometry dictated by the warp and the weft in combination with the free painterly possibilities of screen-printing, Guermonprez created fiber wall hangings rich in texture and delicate in line. The mood and style of her work reflect the climatic environment of the San Francisco area where she lived and the cultural impress of Oriental art and thought that continues to influence the work of so many California craftsmen.

74

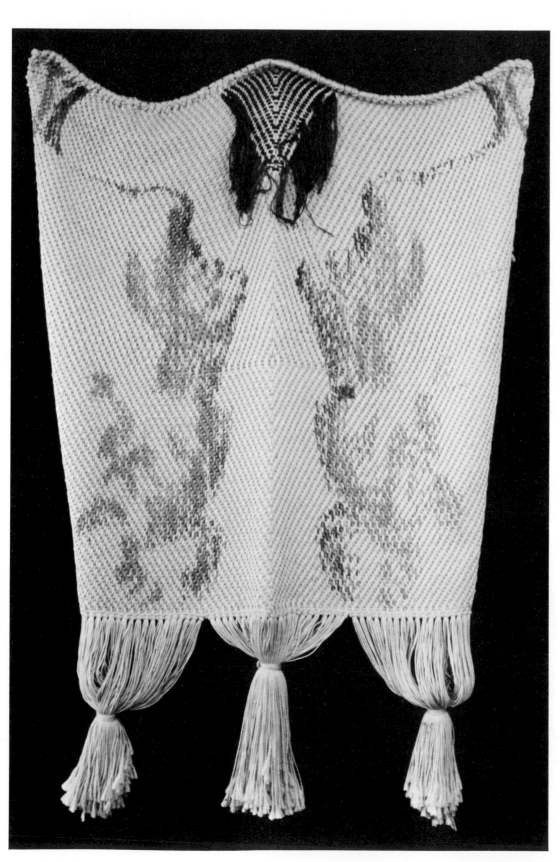

75. Tapestry. Trude Guermonprez. 1973. Approx. 36″ x 24″. Photograph by Michael Hall.

76. Tapestry. Trude Guermonprez. 1974. 36″ x 48″. Photograph by Michael Hall.

77. *Calico Falls*. Jar. Wayne Higby. 1973. Raku-fired earthenware. H. 13″; W. 13″; D. 11″.

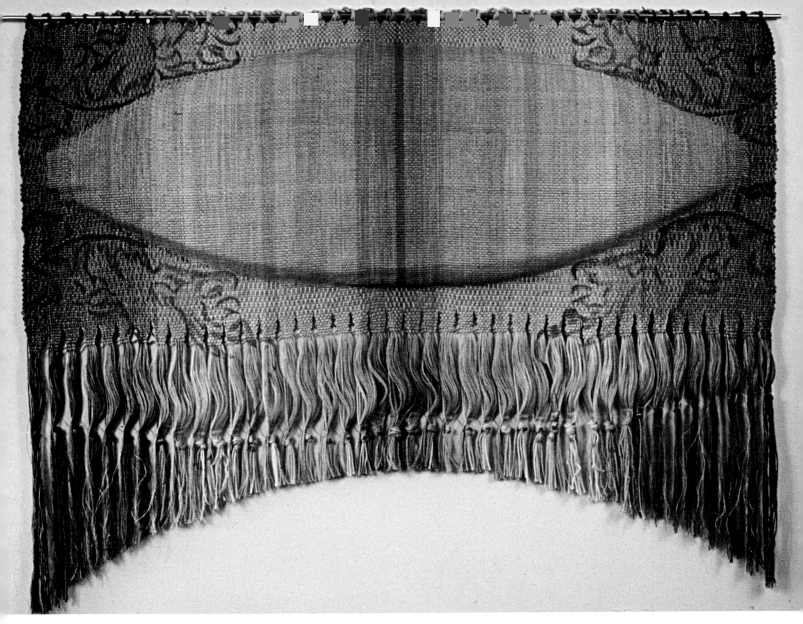

76

77

78. *Our Mountains.*
Tapestry. Trude
Guermonprez. 1971. Woven
with screen printing.
60″ x 44″. (Mrs. Olive
Cowell)

79. *Gift for Nothing.*
Knotted form. Neda Al-
Hilali. 1975. Variety of fibers.
8″ x 5″. (D. Lance Stewart)

The style statement of the contemporary fine craftsman is broad and varied. Today the influence that once flowed only from Europe to America has started to flow both ways. It is the fine craftsman who is the foremost beneficiary of this new international hybridization of the crafts. The tradition of elegance is becoming international in our time, and American craftsmen are substantially affecting the way in which this tradition expands.

The aesthetic of today's fine craftsman is a dialogue between ideas and materials. History and technology continue to influence this dialogue. The basic skills used in metalworking, pottery making, glassblowing, weaving, and woodworking are relearned by each generation. Today, however, new materials and very sophisticated processes for shaping them challenge the imagination of the modern craftsman and keep today's fine craft output truly creative. In linking a deep-rooted respect for traditional workmanship to a healthy curiosity about the expressive potentials to be found in new materials and methods, the fine craftsman in America sustains and extends the tradition of elegance.

79

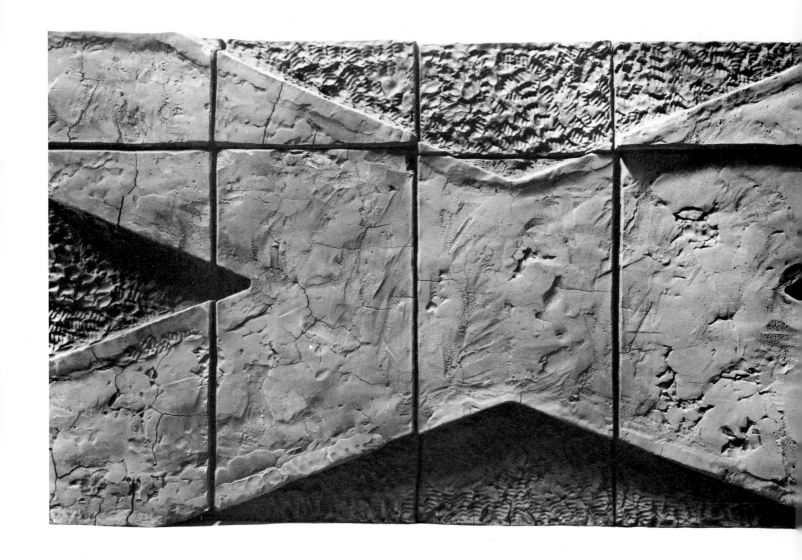

80. *Wall-X*. John Mason.
1965. Firebrick.
7'1½" x 14'6" x 18". Photograph by Frank J. Thomas.

TOWARD ABSTRACTION

Albers
Autio
Cohn
Elliott
Farrell
Hilton
Hopkins
Hughto
Hui
Kaneko
Lipofsky
Little

Littleton
Mason
Myers
Neri
Rapoport
Rossbach
Sekimachi
Voulkos

81. *Red Meander*. Tapestry. Anni Albers. 1954. 27″ x 21″. Photograph by De Cusati.

82 (Overleaf, page 78). *Anatom*. Peter Voulkos. 1973. Stoneware. H. 41″. Photograph by Paul Kennedy. (Estelle E. Friedman, Julie and Michael Hall)

83 (Overleaf, page 79). Vase form. Peter Voulkos. 1973. Stoneware and porcelain. H. 32″. Photograph by Michael Hall.

The aesthetic issues that have stimulated modern craftsmen have come from many sources. The modernist tradition in painting emerges as a major influence in much American craftwork. The relationship among painters, sculptors, and craftsmen is little understood, but has clearly been significant throughout most of the twentieth century. The issue of abstraction has dominated post-Bauhaus crafts, as the sophistication of the craftsman has moved in step with the escalating sophistication of modern art in general.

Cubism and its offshoots can be traced as the roots of most abstraction in modern painting. In the crafts, however, an abstract form vocabulary based on simple patterns and shapes has existed for thousands of years. The flat "plane" space celebrated by Picasso in his Synthetic Cubist period has always been basic to the weaver's art. The elegant geometric patterns of Paul Klee's painting are paralleled in the decorated pottery of many African tribes as well as that of the American Indian. Georges Rouault understood this historic abstraction in the crafts and took inspiration for his bold style of painting from early stained-glass windows executed by the master glassworkers of medieval Europe.

The urbanization of the craft movement in the twentieth century brought the interaction between painting and the crafts to an interface that was far from casual or coincidental. The Bauhaus consciously worked toward a broad synthesis of the arts. Bauhaus weavers and designers worked hand in hand with painters and architects to shape a style that drew heavily on the lessons of modern abstract art. Craftsmen in this period saw the forms of their primitive or folk history suddenly integrated into the most sophisticated advanced art and design styles of the time. The general acceptance of abstraction in modern art suddenly created a new viability for the craftsman's work. This fact brought the craft community into its modern consciousness of style and stylistic evolution, and permanently linked American crafts to the arts of painting and architecture.

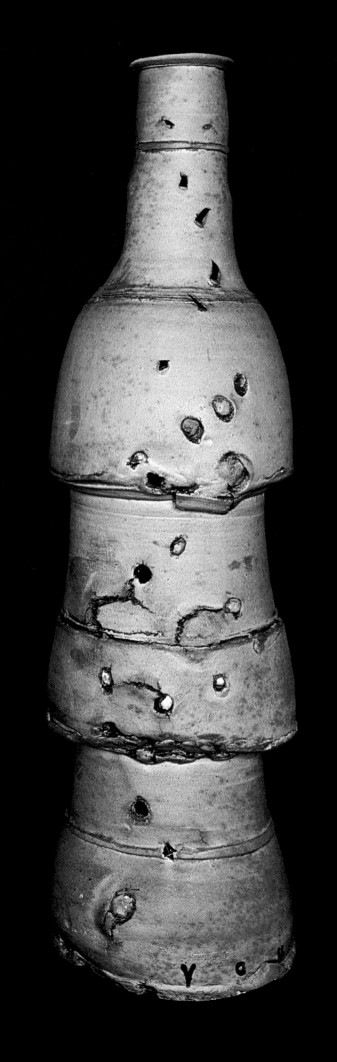

83

84

84. Plate. Peter Voulkos. 1973. Stoneware and porcelain. Diam. 18″. Photograph by The Schopplein Studios. Photograph courtesy Quay Gallery. (Rose Slivka)

85. Tapestry. Anni Albers. 1927. 72″ x 48″. (Busch-Reisinger Museum, Harvard University)

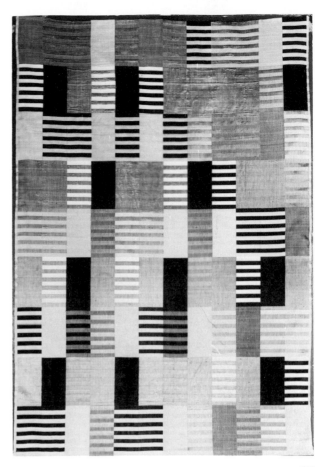

85

The weaving of Anni Albers typifies the emergence of abstraction in modern crafts. Her work, although conceived as a textile statement, is highly pictorial in its visual aspect. Albers utilizes the intrinsic geometric vigor of the warp and the weft as the foundation for building a personal abstraction of shape and color imposed on a fiber plane. Her wall hangings reflect the sophistication of an author fully aware of the work of Piet Mondrian, Georges van Tongerloo, and the architects, Gerrit Rietveld and Walter Gropius. As an early instructor at the Black Mountain College in North Carolina, Anni Albers brought the message of abstraction to an eager group of students who affected a dramatic change in the outlook of the American craftsman.

Abstraction in American painting came into its own with the Abstract Expressionist movement of the 1950s in New York. The generation of painters that included Jackson Pollock, Franz Kline, and Willem de Kooning developed a style of art that radicalized the concept of *abstraction* with its spontaneity, improvisation, and energy. The built-up textures of Pollock, the powerful calligraphy of Kline, and the brutal color of de Kooning struck a responsive chord in the American craft community, which soon reverberated with its own expressionistic tone.

No single figure brought more to the expressionist movement in the crafts than ceramist Peter Voulkos. His slashed
and splattered stoneware plates and brutal sculptured jars
have left an indelible imprint on the history of pottery. For
Voulkos, clay and the Abstract Expressionist view were perfect complements. The so-called action painters sought to
approach their work with total spontaneity, expressing the
unconscious self in a flurry of marks and strokes. Coaxing and
forcing clay to its limits, Voulkos brilliantly extended the
expressionist vocabulary into monolithic sculptural forms,
which he gouged and cut and then enlivened with splashes of
colored slip and glaze. Both the form and surface of a Voulkos piece capture the sense of gesture so critical to the
expressionist style.

Typical of the abstractionists in the contemporary
craft world, Voulkos endeavored to blend his craft tradition
with the fine arts tradition. His genius allowed him to combine his profound understanding of Japanese pottery with
an equally insightful interpretation of Picasso's painting and
Kline's spirit. For Voulkos, this union bore a creative realization that transcended derivation to become a powerful art
statement in its own right.

Beginning as an Abstract Expressionist, ceramist John
Mason evolved a clay expression closely tied to the Minimal
and Systemic movements of the mid-1960s. His large slab-
built boxes have a primal essence influenced more by the
intellectual and contemplative values of the Minimalists
than by the painterly involvements of the Abstract Expres-
sionists. Recently, Mason has been constructing symmetrical
configurations of stacked firebricks. This new work is a
form of refined abstraction at architectural scale that in-
vestigates structure and pattern rather than the plastic
aesthetics of clay. There is something meditative and poetic
about Mason's new firebrick constructions. They seem like
perfectly preserved architectural fragments left by an ancient
civilization of builders.

87

88

88. *Loops No. 2.* Manuel Neri. 1961. Ceramic. H. 18½". Photograph by Michael Hall. (Peter Voulkos)

89. *Grand Rapids.* John Mason. 1973. Firebrick. 25½" x 25'10½" x 72". Photograph by Michael Hall.

Jun Kaneko shapes clay into linear constructions touched by a very lyric view of forms as environment. His early works from the 1960s looped and zigzagged across the floor. Boldly striped and brightly colored, these early pieces had a beguiling "pop" sort of presence that nonetheless remained totally abstract and self-referential. Recently, Kaneko's work has involved constructions of long, brittle clay bars shaped in self-supporting stacks. These stacks, both singly and in combination, are cages or barricades that create environments and modify architectural interiors.

89

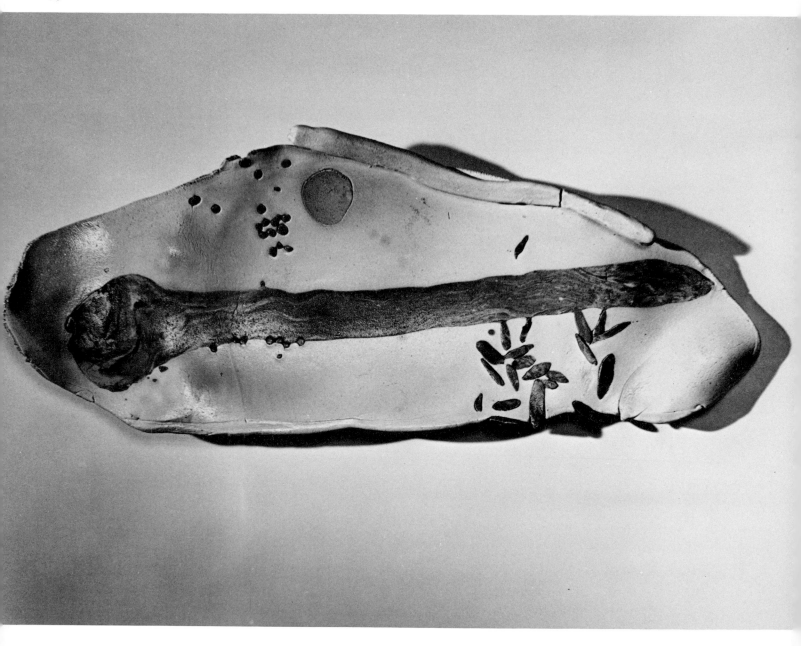

90. *Push Through*. Margie Hughto. 1972. Salt-glazed colored porcelain. 11″ x 25″. (Artist's collection)

91. *Tapestry Net*. Lillian Elliott. 1972. Cotton strips, wool, and nylon net. 32″ x 38″; Photograph by Karel Bauer.

92. *The Idaho Hills Vessel*. Jar. Rudy Autio. 1963. Hand-built stoneware. H. 16″. Photograph by Michael Hall. (Fred Marer)

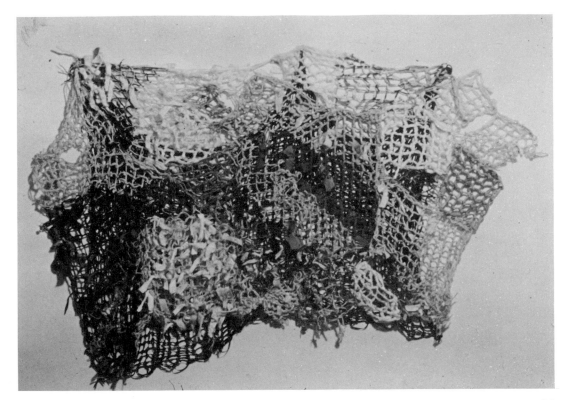

91

92

93. *Ceramic Form*. Ka Kwong Hui. 1976. Ceramic, glazed red, black, white, and gold. 30″ x 22″.

94. *Sanbon Ashi*. Jun Kaneko. 1969. Clay. 19″ x 30″ x 72″.

94

93

95

96

95. *Bisque Clay Rods*. Bill
Farrell. 1976. Clay. 3′ x 12′.
(The Art Institute of
Chicago)

96. Untitled. Jun Kaneko.
1974. Clay. 26″ x 26″ x 26″.

97. *Situation with Lariat*.
Ken D. Little. 1973–1974.
Ceramic, rope, water. H. 50″.
(Artist's collection)

97

98. *Glass Spectrum*. Harvey
K. Littleton. 1974. Stained
cathedral glass. 32″ x 26″ x 6″.
Photograph by John Littleton.

99. *Linear Loops*. Harvey
K. Littleton. 1976. Blown
glass. 10″ x 9″ x 3″ and
13″ x 7½″ x 3″. Photograph
by John Littleton.

98

99

100

101

102

Many contemporary glassworkers have been involved with issues of abstraction from the outset. Glass innovator Harvey Littleton has always been fascinated with the pure color properties of his medium. His constructions in glass rods and plate glass are literally painted in a full spectrum of subtle color, refracted and diffused through the glass itself. The color intensity of Littleton's work rivals that found in the work of the contemporary color-field painters Morris Louis and Kenneth Noland. Like these painters, Littleton seeks a form of abstraction in which light and color become both the content and the form of a new aesthetic.

Glassblower Marvin Lipofsky, who once studied with Littleton, has pursued an abstraction based in the tradition of functional glassblowing and figurative sculpture. Lipofsky's Rubensesque forms have a full-blown sensuality that pulses through the candy stripes and metallic iridescences that wrap around their surfaces. Lipofsky has collaborated with master glassworkers all over the world who have assisted him in the execution of the complex and exacting pieces he has designed. Through these collaborations Marvin Lipofsky has perfected an ultrarefined abstraction enhanced by the full range of the glassblower's craft.

100. *Venini Series.* Glass sculpture. Marvin Lipofsky. 1972. H. 12″; W. 14″. Photograph by Marvin Lipofsky. (Private collection)

101. *Pink Sea.* Eric Hilton. 1970–1971. Glass, wood, plastic. 48″ x 48″ x 18″. Photograph by Eric Hilton.

102. *Space Cup #18.* Michael Cohn. 1975. Blown, cut, and fabricated glass. H. 8″. Photograph by Michael Hall.

103. *Nuutajärbi-Sumi,* Finland series. Glass sculpture. Marvin Lipofsky. 1970. Blown glass. W. 28″. Photograph by Marvin Lipofsky. (Artist's collection)

104. *Flower.* Joel Philip Myers. 1974. White opal glass. 8¼″ x 5″.

105. Chair with coffee table (tripod base). Jack Rogers Hopkins. 1974. Cherrywood. H. 28″. Photograph by Richard Gross. (Mr. and Mrs. John V. Wise)

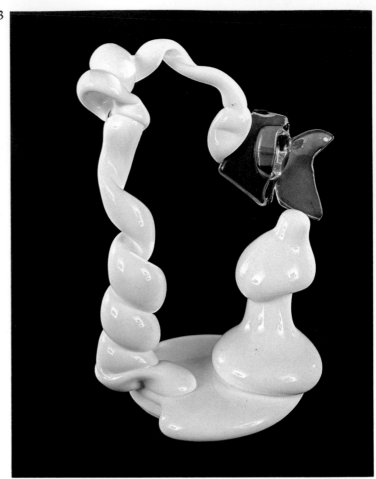

103

104

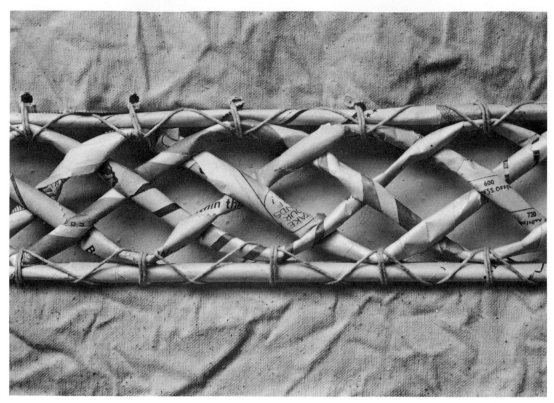

106

Ed Rossbach, working in Berkeley, California, is an influential abstractionist in the field of fiber work. His art is committed to conceptualization rather than technical manipulation. He feels that technique per se can be a barrier to personal expression. He utilizes nonfiber materials such as newspaper and plastic in conjunction with traditional weaving and basketmaking. Rossbach's knowledge of fiber history is extensive, and he employs many ancient forms in the making of his own containers and wall pieces. His weavings seem like fragments, old and yet new, simple and yet intellectually sophisticated. His provocative work emphasizes the strong abstract patterns of interlacing horizontals, verticals, and diagonals that come from the weaving process itself. Ed Rossbach's understanding of creativity and its relationship to craft has helped bring about the merging of art and craft.

The evolution of abstraction in art has recently focused on an investigation of what has been labeled *process* and *conceptual* art. Berkeley-based fiber artist, Debra Rapoport, has launched a series of performances and Happenings focused on fiber and textile experiences. Rapoport's early and best-known works are tuniclike garments that she creates to be worn by two or more people. Each garment becomes a flexible bond between the wearers. It moves with them and alters its shape in response to the inevitable concert of physical harmonies and dissonances resulting from the interaction of the wearers. Rapoport's garments become settings for a form of extemporaneous choreography.

106. *Peruvian Shirt*. Ed Rossbach. 1975. Plaited newspaper with canvas. L. 62".

107. *Paperknot*. Ed Rossbach. 1975. Newspaper and plastic knot. L. 50".

107

108. *Fibrous Raiment.*
Debra E. Rapoport. 1969.
Surface-embroidered knitted
environment of mixed yarns.
72″ x 120″. Photograph by
Demetre Lagios.

109. *Silver Squares.* Debra
E. Rapoport. 1973. Knitted
metallic thread and wire,
plastic. 14″ x 12″. Photograph
by Demetre Lagios.

110. *Kemuri Katachi.* Kay
Sekimachi. 1970. Clear nylon
monofilament. 69″ x 10⅛″ x
9⅜″. Photograph by Stone
and Steccati.

More and more creative energy is flowing between the different disciplines of the arts. Picasso, like Peter Voulkos, discovered the expressive potentials of clay. Today, the ceramics of these two artists—one a painter and one a "potter"—have taken their place in the history of art. Likewise, painter Joan Miró and weaver Anni Albers have moved the art of fiber into contemporary art museums around the world. The American craftsman's forty-year probe into a wide gamut of aesthetic concerns has successfully helped to break down the long-standing barriers that once separated fine art and craft. The energy and the talent of craftsmen have become significant factors in today's art equation. American abstract art is the richer for the contributions of artists like Anni Albers, John Mason, and Harvey Littleton. Committed to their own materials, their own disciplines and history, as well as to their particular artistic goals, the abstractionists have brought new vitality and scope to contemporary culture.

108

109

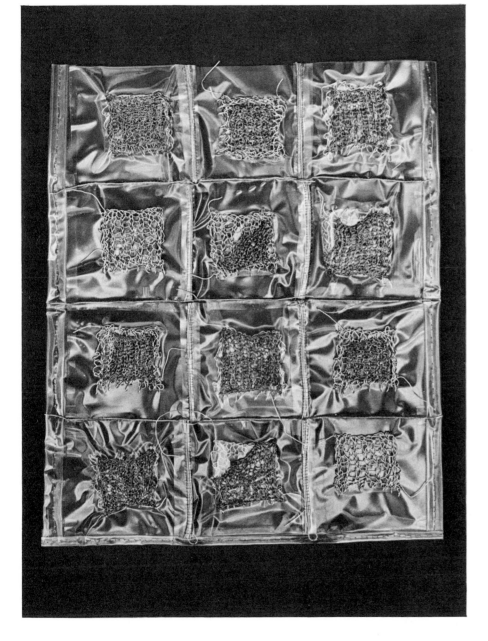

110

A DECADE OF FUNK

Arneson
Bailey
Breschi
Buck
Gilhooly
Melchert
Middlebrook
Price
Rice

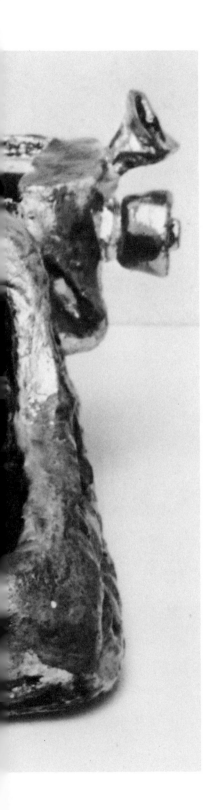

111. *Typewriter*. Robert
Arneson. 1965. Ceramic.
10″ x 12″. Photograph
courtesy Allan Stone Gallery.
(Dr. Ralph Lusskin)

Between 1960 and 1970 the American craft scene was significantly influenced by an aesthetic called "Funk." Funk developed in the San Francisco Bay area of California during the early 1960s as the result of a historic interaction among regional craftsmen, painters, and sculptors.

Funk art was brash, iconoclastic, and highly personal. Peter Selz, in his essay "Funk" (in exhibition catalogue *Funk*, University of California, Berkeley, 1967), wrote: "Funk art is hot rather than cool; it is committed rather than disengaged; it is bizarre rather than formal; it is sensuous; and, frequently, it is quite ugly and ungainly. Although usually three-dimensional, it is non-sculptural in any traditional way and irreverent in attitude."

The work of the Funk artists appeared hastily fashioned and incorporated strange images in highly nonformal arrangements. Funk forms were erratic. Narrow squiggly lines collided with rigid geometric shapes. Flat planes of colors became bedfellows with jazzy patterns and trompe-l'oeil textures. To move through a Funk composition is to meet the unexpected at every turn. Funk made fun of sex in an unsophisticated manner that was refreshingly nonadult. In fact, Funk was more than an art style: It was a social movement that heckled the sacred and ostracized the conventional in the celebration of a defiant new antitaste art philosophy.

The Funk work of the 1960s found its genesis in the interaction of a group of highly independent clay artists assembled around Peter Voulkos. This group included James Melchert, Robert Arneson, Kenneth Price, and David Gilhooly. Curiously, Voulkos, the formalist and master craftsman, catalyzed a ceramic production that was both antiformal and anticraft. It was Voulkos's energy and openness that supported the Funk spirit and encouraged the Funk ceramic expression that always answered "Why not" to the question "Why?"

112

112. *Elephant Ottoman.*
David Gilhooly. 1966. White
earthenware and vinyl.
H. 16″. Photograph courtesy
The Hansen-Fuller Gallery,
San Francisco.

113. *Ghost Jar with Butter-
flies.* James Melchert. 1964.
Ceramic. 6″ x 6″ x 10″.
Photograph courtesy James
Melchert. (Rene Di Rosa)

114. *27 minutes in the life
of . . .* James Melchert. 1967.
Clay, plywood, earthenware,
and low-fire glaze. 72″ x 72″.
(Mr. and Mrs. Auram
Goldberg)

113

114

115. *"A" for Magritte.* James Melchert. 1970. Earthenware. H. 22″. Photograph by Michael Hall. (Robert Kuykendahl)

116. *R. G. Violet.* Kenneth Price. c. 1967. Ceramic. 5″ x 3½″ x 9″. Photograph by Michael Hall. (Jacqueline Greber)

Voulkos, with his expressionist pottery, had defied and defiled the tradition of clay in the form of pots, and the younger artists simply extended this assault to challenge even the tradition of clay as clay. Clay was the ideal vehicle for both the forms and attitudes of Funk. Clay was quick to work, and the Funk artist utilized this by inventing forms that stated "spontaneity." Clay was adaptable to a range of ideas, and the surface of clay could be glazed, painted, flocked, or even embellished with decals. Funk pointed out new directions for the use of clay, and the American craftsman followed these directions with inspiration and zeal.

116

The Funk ceramists were respectful of the Surrealists' use of unfamiliar and unusual objects in inappropriate environments. Surrealist painter Salvador Dali placed clocks and rocks in a dream desert. Funk ceramist James Melchert updated this Surrealist motif by setting an array of inscribed

115

117

clay arches next to a Mickey Mouse head on a checkered game board. What is the game? What are the rules? Are the rules known to Melchert, or are they to be made up arbitrarily by each person who views the game? Perhaps there is no game and the cryptic words and the Mickey Mouse float independently through the checkered field of a dream. In another period Melchert developed a bizarre, grisly form of polychromed clay portraiture that he called "ghost-ware." Half comic strip and half Francis Bacon, these Funk pieces leer with a ghoulish insolence that mocks conventional stereotypes of both art and craft.

Robert Arneson turned his talent to assaulting the tactile senses of the clay world. His ceramic *Typewriter* (1965) slumps with a casual "pop" audacity, but becomes curiously ominous when the viewer realizes that the typewriter keys are tiny female fingertips complete with luster-fired red nails. The Arneson typewriter might well stand as the embodiment of the Funk manifesto. It jolts, intimidates, and assaults the traditional values of art and good taste.

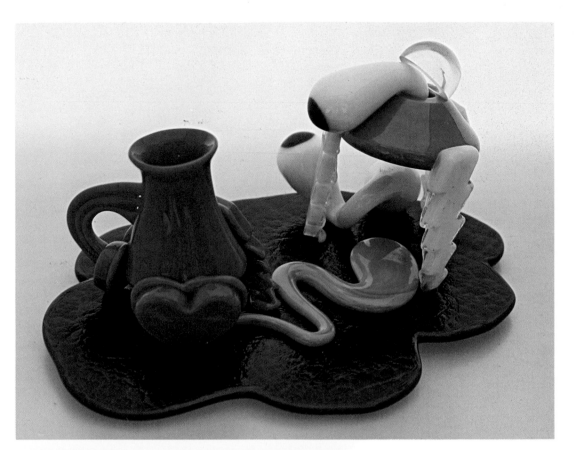

119

120

119. *Cup*. Kenneth Price.
1962–1964. Stoneware.
H. 4″. Photograph by
Michael Hall. (Betty Asher)

120. *Cup*. Al Rice. 1973.
Blown glass and cast glass.
W. approx. 11″. Photograph
by Michael Hall.

121. *Cup*. Al Rice. 1973.
Cast glass and blown glass.
H. approx. 10″. Photograph
by Marvin Lipofsky.

121

Kenneth Price, another strong Funk artist, evolved his pottery into a highly eccentric statement. His cups and peculiar amorphous sculptures are imbued with a sense of mystery. Something enigmatic radiates through the brilliant colors that encase his private, silent world of form. Price rejected traditional glaze surfaces in favor of enamel and lacquer paint, which he brushed and sprayed over his fired clay shapes. This brash innovation was quickly noted and absorbed by the clay community. The expressive vocabulary of the crafts was again extended by the curiosity and courage of one of the Funk innovators.

David Gilhooly, like Price, was not shackled by a traditional view of his medium. His famous *Elephant Ottoman* (1966) combines clay and cloth to produce a funky, funny, absurd monument true to the spirit of Dada.

By the late 1960s, craftsmen had popularized the term *funky* to mean "down-home," "clever," "offhand," and "witty." A second generation of artists began making "funky things" rather than Funk art. More artists brought more diversification to the style and the message of Funk spread across the country. California, however, was still the land of Funk and remained the home for the modern descendants of the Funk family.

122

Clayton Bailey, originally trained in Wisconsin, moved west to become part of a neo-Funk group, the "nut artists." Bailey's art involves a traveling clay performance that incorporates the ballyhoo of an early American patent medicine show with a hilarious spoof on anthropology. Using the pseudonym Dr. Gladstone, Clayton sells clay souvenirs of anthropological finds. The good doctor claims to have "found" the elusive "Big Foot" skeleton. Very few people really want to own the fossilized Big Foot "droppings" that Bailey sells. The show he puts on is part workshop and part Happening, wrapped in a healthy dose of traditional American tongue in cheek humor. Clayton is now busily building his own museum, which will allow the public to see the "Clayolithic" wonders that Dr. Gladstone has unearthed.

123

124

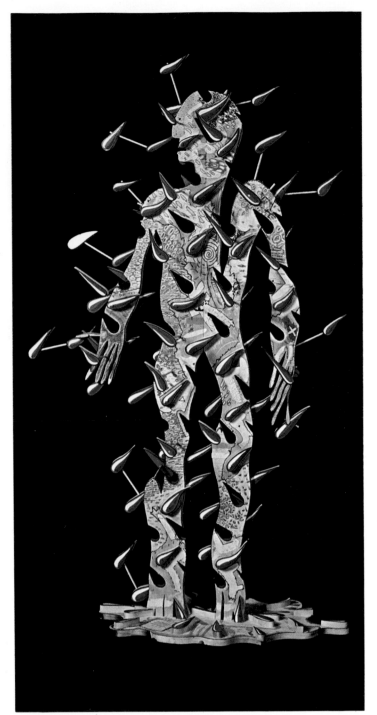

125

126

127

128

127. *Rough Soup Tureen.*
David Middlebrook. 1975.
Thrown and hand-built
ceramic. 16″ x 17″ x 17″.
Photograph by Rick Sfera.
(Private collection)

128. *Oasis Man.* John Buck.
1973. Cast aluminum. H.
87″. (Gerald Hoepfner)

129. *Death Ship.* John Buck.
1973. Pit-fired ceramic
copper wire (fired complete).
L. 16″. (Artist's collection)

The infectious spirit of Funk extends into other disciplines of the crafts. Glassblower Al Rice molds jewel-colored glass into a landscape and then places a staring cartoon eyeball in the middle of his composition, with singularly jarring effect. His work is clearly influenced by Robert Hudson's early Funk metal sculpture. Rice, however, has evolved a style and technique that beautifully adapts his unique images to the special qualities of blown and molded glass.

Recently, Montana's John Buck, working primarily with wood, has incorporated the tenets of Funk art into his own inventive statement. Buck creates a world of idiosyncratic symbols and comic-strip images. In one construction, he fashions a polychromed silhouette figure helplessly trapped in a barrage of daggerlike raindrops. In another he seems to extend the tradition of Melchert's ghost-ware with a clay canoe filled with gray stonelike forms shrouded in rope netting. This death-ship drifts across the floor like an apparition of some ominous Viking burial. In the best spirit of Funk, Buck's work is both gripping and outrageous—rich in images that call up the hidden and ubiquitous fears and ironies that gnaw at the human psyche.

The *enfants terribles* of Funk thrust a thumb in the eye of tradition and successfully tore down many of the old values that once separated art from craft. Funk, per se, lasted only a decade, but its raw humor and irreverent spirit have proliferated in a variety of directions that sustain an important youthful curiosity and energy in the craft world today.

129

130. *Bud*. Pat Oleszko. 1973. Satin, corduroy, chicken wire, yarn, and Dacron polyester. Photograph by Carl Fisher.

131. *Buddy*. Pat Oleszko. 1973. Satin, corduroy, chicken wire, yarn, and Dacron polyester. Photograph by Carl Fisher.

132. *Buddy Pop*. Pat Oleszko. 1973. Satin, corduroy, chicken wire, yarn, and Dacron polyester. Photograph by Carl Fisher.

133. *Poppy*. Pat Oleszko. 1973. Satin, corduroy, chicken wire, yarn, and Dacron polyester. Photograph by Carl Fisher.

130

131

VISIONS AND FANTASIES

134. *Car Kiln*. Patti Warashina. 1970. Earthenware with underglazes, low-fire and luster glazes, and plaster. L. approx. 32″. (Kohler Collection)

135. *Sinking Ship on a Couch*. Richard Shaw. 1971. Earthenware and acrylics. L. 36″. Photograph courtesy The Hansen-Fuller Gallery. (Rene di Rosa)

136. *Knife on a Board Cup*. Richard Shaw. 1974. Porcelain. L. 9″. Photograph courtesy The Hansen-Fuller Gallery.

In 1919 the French poet, André Breton, began an attempt to extend the arts through a utilization of Sigmund Freud's pioneering research into the workings of the unconscious. Seated in a semidarkened room, he tried to let his mind wander into the dream state and then quickly to write down whatever visual phantoms or illusions had come to him. He sought to enrich the art of poetry with the images of the "inner mind," and in so doing, generated the art form known as Surrealism. The goal of Surrealism, according to Breton, was "... the future resolution of those seemingly contradictory states, dream and reality, in a kind of absolute reality, surreality, so to speak" (Calvin Tomkins and Editors of Time-Life Books, *The World of Marcel Duchamp*, New York: Time Incorporated, 1966). Today Breton's world of the unconscious has become a patrimony for a group of craftsmen who could be called the *imagists*.

134

Like Breton, the imagists are concerned with the creation of a tangible world seen through the veil of the unconscious. Theirs is an art of recognizable content, far removed from the nonreferential forms of abstraction. Animals, trees, and faces tumble through their compositions. All manner of beasts and fantastic things become personal symbols for each artist's own internal reality, in the tradition of Dali, Magritte, and Chagall.

Capricious touches of humor move impishly through the work of the imagists, providing a gentle counterpoint to their bizarre dream images. Like Alexander Calder and Claes Oldenburg, the imagists appreciate the special aesthetic potentials of whimsy and jest. Humor, for the imagists, is something quite different from the humor of the Funk artists. The Funk group used an often raw and ribald humor

135

136

137. *Woman Serving Soup.*
Patti Warashina. 1976.
Earthenware with underglaze
and low-fire glaze. H. 28";
W. 18"; D. 14". Photograph
by Rick Sfera. (Artist's
collection)

138. *Stick.* Light-switch
plate. Pencil Bros. (Ken Cory
and Les LePere). 1974.
Champlevé enamel. 4½" x
2¾" x ¼". (Artist's collection)

139. *Heavenly.* Thomas
Simpson. 1970. Painted wood
and acrylic. H. 60". (Artist's
collection)

137

138

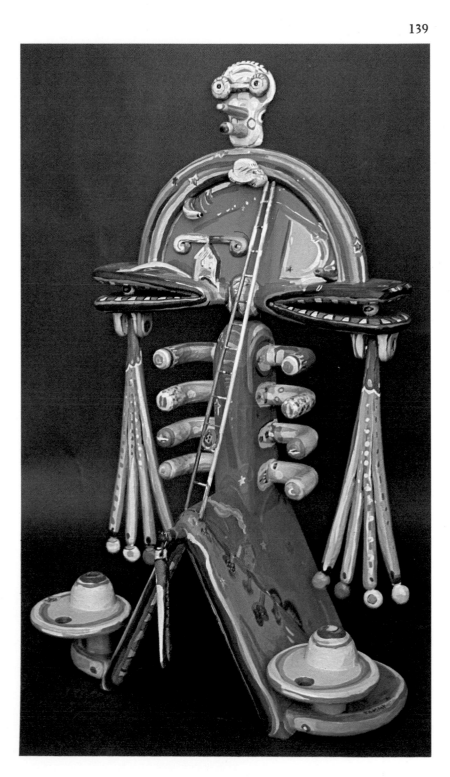

to add discord and cacophony to their work, whereas the imagists delight in punning and in the use of "one-liners" to please rather than to shock. The element of humor keeps the art of the imagists in an equilibrium balanced somewhere between the dark and light sides of life.

Composition, for the imagists, is a counterpoint between symmetry and asymmetry. Within the confines of a serene and classic matrix, shapes often tumble in gleeful disarray, randomly conjured up through Freud's method of "free association." The imagists handle scale and proportion in a manner generally associated with naïve or folk art. A large face is placed next to a tiny tree; a small hand near the voluptuous forms of an overblown odalisque. Irregular proportion metamorphoses the images into the dream world, where things are not always as they seem, where illusion becomes reality and reality, illusion. These images are skillfully manipulated so that their juxtaposition produces a distinct mental jolt. It is the combination of rest and unrest that makes the work of the imagists so fascinating.

Color forms a strong part of the imagist expression. It is used with great vibrancy. Strong primary reds, blues, and yellows add flamboyance and vitality to work that teems with mystery and life. The reddest reds with clashing lipstick pinks and baby blues add energy and potency to the oeuvre. The imagist palette is evolved directly from today's urban genre and pulses with the contradictions and volatility of modern city life.

One of the most innovative craftsmen to work with dream images is Patti Warashina. Since 1965 her art has been involved with fantastic ceramic Rube Goldbergian machines and exaggerated whimsical clay objects. These creations synthesize a bit of Dada with the artist's own Japanese heritage and personal sense of humor. Colorful and exquisitely made, Warashina's jars and absurdist constructions epitomize the aesthetic of the imagists. Her piece, *Car Kiln* (1970), is a fast-moving car made of ceramic brick, with gold luster flames streaming from its windows.

140. *Canopy*. Desk with candle holder. Thomas Simpson. 1974. Pine and acrylic. H. 30". (Fairtree Fine Crafts Institute)

141. *Bird*. Pendant. Pencil Bros. (Ken Cory and Les LePere). 1974. Champlevé enamel and pencils. H. 3½". (Pencil Sisters—Merion Gartler and Marcella Benditt)

142. *Chicken Chairs*. John Bauer. 1973. Rooster: shedira, Japanese oak; Hen: Japanese oak. H. approx. 47".

140

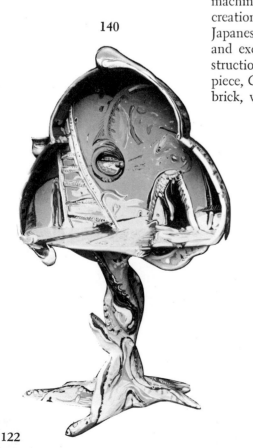

141

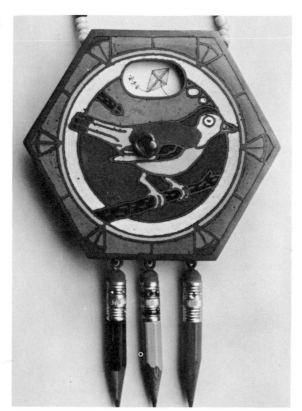

142

143

144

145

The title, *Car Kiln*, is a bit of camp wordplay alluding to a type of pottery kiln that utilizes a wheel-mounted floor for the easy loading and firing of ceramic ware. The title of the piece completes a pun that sets *Car Kiln* up as an in-group rebus especially humorous to all those intimate with the potter's world. Warashina's art, in the best Surrealist tradition, is an art of words and pictures. Its strength of form and idea has influenced countless clay artists all over the United States for more than a decade.

Richard Shaw's ceramics are filled with nostalgia and puzzlement. Shaw juxtaposes disparate objects precariously balanced in enigmatic relationships. His constructions seem to actualize, in three dimensions, vistas drawn from the surreal landscape of the mind. In one piece Shaw creates the absurd image of the ill-fated *Titanic* taking a nose dive into an overstuffed couch. In another he constructs an elaborate cup by setting a burlap-imprinted cylinder on a slab supporting a checkered porcelain napkin and trompe-l'oeil pocketknife. Concentrating on the visual ambivalence that can come from the restructuring of material objects from everyday life, Shaw has been an important link between the Funk movement and the younger generation of imagists.

Many of the imagists create objects rooted in traditional, functional craft vocabularies. Function, however, is often disguised, and it takes some close observation to discover the well-engineered clasp of a pendant or the lid of a covered jar fashioned in the imagist idiom.

Thomas Simpson transforms usable furniture into bizarre grotesqueries of shape and image. His calls his work "fantasy furniture." Although his cradles, chairs, and dressers are functional, this fact is obscured by a transmutation of their form into the realm of the fantastic and the absurd. A simple coffee table becomes a landscape, a candle holder becomes a weird figure with glassy eyes. Assaulting the orthodoxy of natural wood finishes, he paints his forms with writhing patterns of twisting lines that delineate both the abstract and figural aspects of his images. There is nothing easy or tasteful in Simpson's statement. In fact, it seems that he has chosen to use the art of furniture making as a means of expressing a highly personalized surreal aesthetic.

Ken Cory and Les LePere work under the joint alias of the Pencil Brothers. They fashion imaginative pendants, buckles, and light switches with rich enamel work on copper. They delight in transforming simple, useful objects into magical, fabulous miniature paintings. They juxtapose unrecognizable objects with common images such as horses, tableware, or birds floating together in a pictorial space flattened with planes of intense color and delineated by clean, geometric lines.

Woodworker John Bauer's regal chairs seem like thrones surviving from some extinct pagan culture. Inlaying woods of contrasting grains and colors, Bauer ornaments his chairs with strange mythical animals, delicate butterflies, and human figures of recondite origin. One minute these images are isolated in exquisite inlaid cameos, the next they are fused with the forms of the chair itself, twisting with primitive intensity around its massive arms and back. Inspired by Victorian furniture, Chinese bronzes, and early Pennsylvania cast iron, Bauer creates unusual furniture ideas for his own time.

The imagist expression always has a very private side. Fiber artist Jon Riis and metalworker Richard Mafong, working in collaboration, have created their own fanciful race of little people woven from colored yarn and dressed in hammered silver costumes. Their gleeful, voluptuous women are encased in carapacelike shapes, creating a rich formal contrast between soft fiber forms and rigid metal armor. Combining their virtuoso talents in tapestry-weave,

146

146. *Elephant Teapot*. Ann Adair. 1968. Porcelain, with quilted cozy by Marina Bebee. H. 9″. Photograph by Michael Hall. (Mrs. Martin Luther King, Jr.)

147. *Doll*. Richard Mafong and Jon Riis. 1975. Metallic threads with tapestry weave, silver, ivory, and bronze. Metal cover: 4″ x 4″. (Artist's collection)

148. *Doll* (with metal cover removed). Richard Mafong and Jon Riis. 1975. Metal cover: 4″ x 4″. (Artist's collection)

147

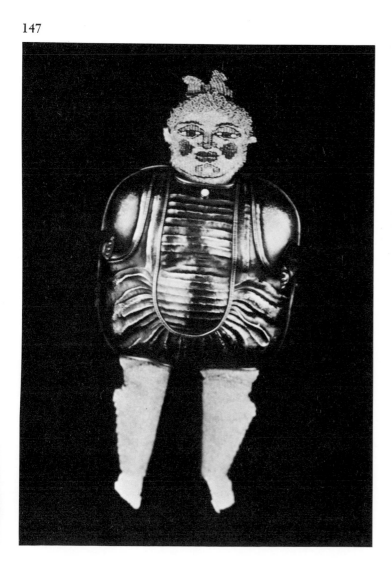

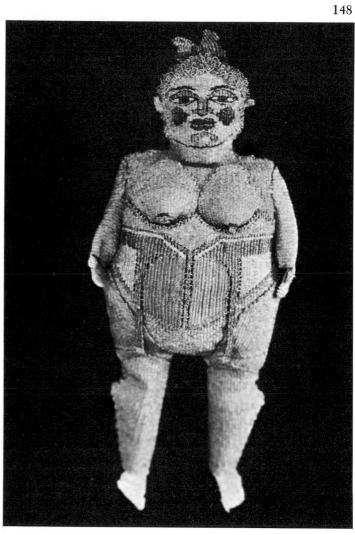

149

150

149. *Charles Patless.* Pat Oleszko. 1976. Satin, polyester, Dacron, and imitation fur. Photograph by Neil Selkirk.

150. *Two Halves Make a Season* (detail). Lynn Mauser-Bain. 1973. Silk-screened on cloth and trapunto stuffed. 40″ x 110″. (Artist's collection)

151. *Il Papa Nòmina Trenta Cardinali.* Window. Richard Posner. 1975. Leaded glass. 30″ x 40″. Photograph by Pat Gouduis. (Artist's collection)

151

repoussé, and casting, Mafong and Riis achieve a colorful, mirthful expression tempered by a note of seriousness. Are their tiny people caricatures of humanity, or are they smiling imps brought to life from fairy tales? Behind their beguiling smiles, the Mafong-Riis Lilliputians remain mysterious and obscure.

Pat Oleszko goes public with her art, covered head to toe in an array of outrageous costumes. With only a sewing machine she is able to transform herself into anything. Oleszko slips into one of her many costumes, such as "Rachel Tension" or "Charles Patless," and goes into the streets of New York City to execute pieces of impromptu theatre. She may parade as a whiskey sour or even a poppy, doing whatever the costume and the moment suggest to her. The muscle man, "Charles Patless," spoofs the Charles Atlas physical-fitness, body-development cult. The "Patless" costume transforms artist Oleszko into a shimmering mass of knotted satin biceps and bumpy overstuffed deltoids that loom above trim, bronzed gluteus maximus. The effect is wildly funny and carries with it a social comment that convicts Americans of taking themselves and their bodies too seriously. Oleszko's fantastic costumes launched into the "theatre" of the street provide one artist with a thoroughly enjoyable means of bringing her singular, wacky philosophy of life to the American public.

The imagists weave a strange and playful sorcery. Demons and Dada, pranks and Pop—new mischief and mystery from the legacy of André Breton. Surrealism's new child has engendered a spirit of one-upmanship throughout its ranks. Idea and spin-off, pun and comeback—an inside art form that is attracting an ever-expanding audience. Tapping the private resources of the imagination, the imagists create new and compelling statements that confirm the value of the artist in today's world. The visions and fantasies of the imagists exude a spirit that reflects the basic positivism of the American craftsman and the ongoing vitality of new directions in American art.

ICONS FOR OUR TIME

Carpenter   Shawcroft
De Vore   Smith
Di Mare   Tawney
Fenster   Turner
Harper
Jacobs
Nottingham

153. *Bird Shrine* (detail). Walter Nottingham. 1973. Mixed fiber, feathers, beadwork, bones. 72″ x 36″ x 18″. Photograph by J. Douglas Smith. (Robert L. Pfannebecker)

154. *Ashanti*. Robert Turner. 1974. Ceramic. 12″ x 10″. Photograph by Linn Underhill.

155. *Niger #1*. Robert Turner. 1974. Ceramic. H. 12″; W. 17″. Photograph by Rick Sfera. (Robert L. Pfannebecker)

The problems of postindustrial society have been met by craftsmen in many different ways. Aware of the runaway materialism of our culture, the artists in this chapter have committed themselves to a search for personal iconography that recaptures the elusive potency of spiritual energy in art. These artists could be called the *icon makers* because they focus their creative involvement on the making of objects that are vested with arcane magic and unfettered primitive beauty.

In every culture there have always been icons and artists who made them. Historically, icon makers gave their people symbols of power, beauty, and strength through images that were accepted as insights into the enigmas of life. The very word *icon* calls to mind quiet, votive images, mesmerizing in their appearance and haunting in their intensity. Today's icon makers create all manner of objects that are linked to a common motive—the formulation of visual archetypes that encapsulate the most profound life experiences and intuitive wisdoms of man. They offer their work as ritual objects or as objects of contemplation intended to allow pragmatic, corporate modern man to touch his metaphysical self.

Although the work of the modern icon makers has evolved from the fine craft tradition, it is clearly linked to values that are functional rather than decorative. The notion of function usually calls for a special performance required

154

155

156. Basket. Ferne Jacobs. 1972. Rayon straw and polished linen. H. 6″; Diam. 7″. (Katherine Tremaine)

157. Bowl. Richard E. De Vore. 1976. Ceramic. W. 9¾″.

158. *Inner Tube*. Barbara Shawcroft. 1974. Sisal rope, knotless netting. 120″ x 48″. Photograph by Michael Hall.

159. *Gracilis*. Barbara Shawcroft. 1971. Synthetic rope, netting technique. H. 120″. Photograph by Michael Bry. (Artist's collection)

158

159

of an object involved with a specific activity. In traditional use crafts, clay jars "function" as the storage places for foodstuffs, and woven ponchos "function" as coverings for the body. The work of today's icon makers, although not useful in this sense, nonetheless "functions" in the same way that the beaded rattle of an Indian shaman functioned in other times. The shaman's rattle did no ordinary work. But ceremonially, spiritually, and symbolically it rendered a very specific service for the tribal society that knew and appreciated its use. Contemporary icon makers have projected a spiritual need for the things they make, and have built a strong aesthetic around objects created to perform metaphysical functions. Beyond the criteria of design, and far from the mode of style, today's icon makers create works that are perceived as beautiful because they evoke archetypal myths and meanings reaching back to the dawn of human history.

The primitive and the poetic have always fascinated potter Robert Turner. He discovered these qualities in his early study of Japanese pottery, and this influence is still seen in his work. In 1972 Turner's quest for the unselfconscious in art took him to Nigeria. There he felt firsthand the rhythms of African tribal life, and he returned to his studio at Alfred University to begin a series of works embodying much of what he knows of ceremonial icons and mystic symbolisms. His blackened jars, occasionally marked with cryptic symbols that recall ritual scars, compel reverence and contemplation from all who view them. These mystical vessels synthesize the meditative, the spiritual, and the primal applications of the potter's craft.

160. Untitled. Dominic
Di Mare. 1973. Handmade
paper, balsa wood, porcupine
quills. 14½″ x 10½″.
Photograph by Michael Hall.
(Artist's collection)

161. *Red Sea.* Lenore
Tawney. 1974. Red linen.
84″ x 84″. Photograph by
Clayton J. Price. Photograph
courtesy Dextra Frankel.
(Private collection)

161

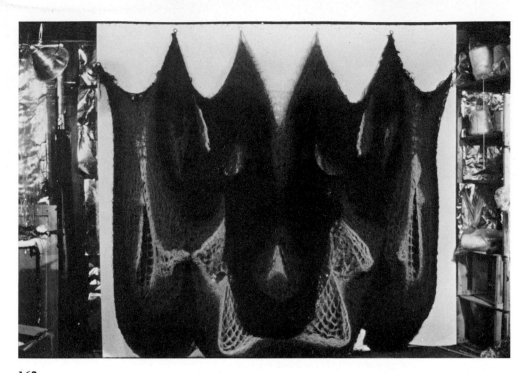

162

162. *Stromboli*. Sherri Smith. 1974. Mohair. 96″ x 96″.

163. *That Other Sea*. Collage. Lenore Tawney. 1966. Antique torn papers and strips of printed text. H. 10⅜″; W. 11″. Photograph by Clayton J. Price. Photograph courtesy Dextra Frankel. (Private collection)

Weaver Lenore Tawney has created fiber works that have immeasurably influenced American weavers for twenty-five years. Very early in her career Tawney became involved with weavings that dealt with monumental-scale iconography. Her expression has always been moody and mystical like that of painters Adolph Gottlieb and Ad Reinhardt. She generally uses a restrained color palette of earth tones to give a simplicity and solemnity to her work. Modulating areas of dense weave with semipermeable passages of single fiber strands, Tawney suggests the freedom and the limitations of life. She sometimes incorporates paper, shells, or bones in her weavings with a spontaneity usually associated with collage. These *objets trouvés* bring a consciousness of the fragility and temporality of living things. She repeatedly utilizes the cruciform and the circle as symbols of man's inner struggle for purity and completeness. In truth, like Mark Rothko's paintings, Tawney's art is an allegory about the mystery and beauty of life.

Woven baskets served ancient man for the storage and transportation of all kinds of commodities. For icon maker Ferne Jacobs, the basket becomes a symbolic container for gathering and protecting the essence of life. Jacobs has revived the art of basketry to create an art that is both formal and sensuous. Her baskets seem like fragile nests built from tightly intertwined linen, wool, and metallic threads. With their wedges and bands of bold color, Ferne Jacobs's basket icons integrate craft, history, lore, and art.

The icon makers frequently search for materials that have been integral to ritual objects of so-called primitive cultures. Their art is highly influenced by the wood and feather masks of the Eskimo, the bone and leather amulets of the Plains Indian, and the bead- and shell-bedecked fetishes of the Pende. The icon makers utilize clay, fur, feathers, fiber, bones, and pebbles as transcendent symbols of universal powers.

163

164

165

166

167

The work of metalworker William Harper exemplifies the contemporary icon maker's use of materials. Harper creates unusual fetish objects that combine technically complex cloisonné enamelwork and fine metal casings with delicate shells, feathers, and simple stones. Harper's work, with its inclusion of animal forms and found things, recalls the cult objects of the Songe and the amulets of the Negere. Using such titles as *Rain Rattle* and *Rattle for a White Witch*, Harper further evokes an aura of unique ceremonial power in his statement.

The process involved in the shaping of an image is particularly important to the icon makers. For many of them, the potency of the final object is ensured through the almost ritual observation of a sequence of acts leading to the completion of the piece. Materials are gathered and prepared in an almost ceremonial manner. Their work spaces or studios become consecrated chambers awaiting the creative impulse. The icon makers work at a pace that is never rushed. Their work process is by nature additive, and each element or form incorporated into an object becomes, in turn, an armature supporting what is added next. Work itself becomes a votive act, as each fiber, stone, bone, or shell is offered toward the materialization of the artist's metaphysical reality.

Dominic Di Mare's *Song Bird Books* (1975) radiate an intensity that confirms the ritual process of all aspects of their creation, from the making of the book paper to the final tying of the binding strings. These small delicate stacks of paper support precious offerings—the tiny, bleached bone of a bird, the quills of a porcupine, or a fishing lure made by the artist's grandfather. Di Mare's imagination leaves behind a masterful display of creation and control. The *Song Bird Books* synthesize pure formal design with a subjective stream of consciousness. The pristine format of the books somehow radiates an aura that captures a fugitive essence of existence and time. Di Mare composes a narrative of the ebb and flow of life and death in the cyclical movements of the universe. He shapes this narrative into a visual poetry that is distinctly his own.

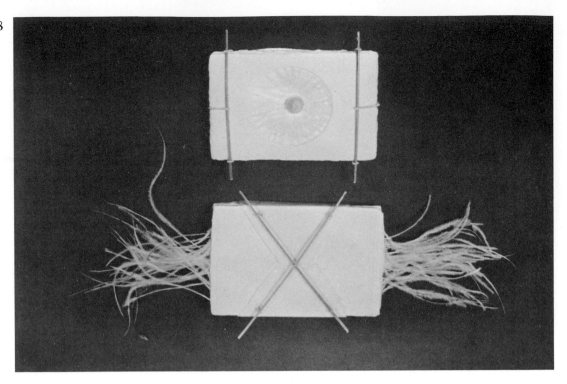

Color plays another distinct role in the expression of the icon makers. In the best sense, this role is largely a symbolic one. Seeking essentiality in their work, the icon makers employ an earthy palette to reflect the eternal substance and grandeur of nature. They offset this palette with dyed fibers of dark purples, iron reds, and saturated ochres to denote man's several connate temperaments—his energy, violence, and splendor.

Utilizing forms and colors reminiscent of the armorial ensigns of the Plains Indians, Walter Nottingham's large fiber works pulse with haunting rhythms. His shieldlike forms are laden with long wool fringes that drape toward the floor with menacing pent-up energy. Each piece becomes a sort of shrine built around a core of twisted or wrapped fiber forms. Part war shield and part headdress, Nottingham's icons exude an enigmatic mystique. Discussing his motivations in *Objects U.S.A.* (1970), Nottingham says: "I am not trying to make the visible seen, but the unseen visible." The essence of his art seeks that aspect of humanity that, at its most savage, is yet quite beautiful.

Today's craftsmen have all grown to their artistic maturity in a world where one human error can trigger the end of civilization as we know it. Artists like Robert Turner, Ferne Jacobs, and Dominic Di Mare have committed their talents to the affirmation of the persistence of life. Their work stands as a forceful testimony to the endurance of the human spirit. Today's icon makers have developed some of the most sophisticated work in the field of contemporary crafts and have revived a compelling aesthetic that has entered the contemporary art arena on its own terms.

168. *Song Bird Book* (two from a series). Dominic Di Mare. 1973. Handmade paper, feathers, sticks. 6" x 3½" (each section). Photograph by Michael Hall. (Private collection)

169. *Song Bird Book* (one from a series). Dominic Di Mare. 1973. Handmade paper, feathers, bones. 6" x 3½" (paper unit). Photograph by Michael Hall. (Private collection)

170. *The Bird Meets with Misfortune Through Flying.* James Carpenter. 1975. Sheet glass, cast glass, and photo emulsion. H. 75". Photograph by Morgan Rockhill. (Artist's collection)

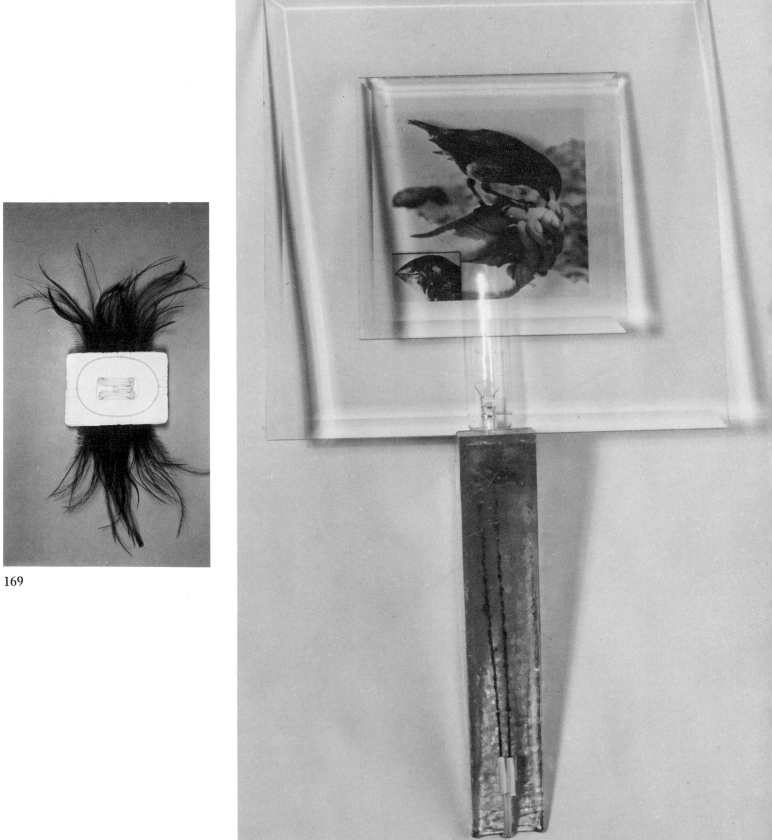

169

170

IDENTITY AND ISSUE

Foster
Frimkess
Griffin
Loloma
Scherr

171. *Blue Whale*. Larry
Foster. 1970. Stained glass
illuminated from within.
L. 108″. Photograph courtesy
"General Whale." ("General
Whale")

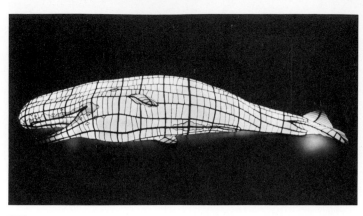

172

173

For over a decade the rising American social awareness that questioned and reshaped so many institutions and values in the United States has given a new shape to American crafts. The activism of the 1960s found a voice in the crafts just as it did in music and so many other popular arts. By 1970 it was clear that a growing number of contemporary craftsmen were turning their skills to creating new expressions that voiced their assessments of many different aspects of American life. Although diversified in their involvements, these artists nonetheless share this chapter under the common designation of the *advocates*, for they share a common commitment to shaping art forms around basic concerns of identity and issue.

Looking back through history, it is clear that artists from many cultures have attempted to interpret the human condition on levels ranging from the most personal to the epic. Francisco Goya's famous series of prints entitled *Disasters of War* chillingly illustrate war as an inferno that brutalizes man to the point where he can commit the most grotesque and savage acts against his own kind. Jacques Louis David's poignant painting *The Death of Marat* became a rallying point for the French Revolution, and stands today as a universal insight into the terrible responsibilities of leadership and a reminder of the very deadly hazards that can beset those who assume it. In the early part of this century, Picasso's monumental *Guernica* (1937) mural became a prophetic signal of the approaching horrors of world war. Using the full brilliance of his post-Cubist style of abstraction, Picasso contorted and distorted his figures in a frightening narrative expressing the pain and confusion of the defenseless Spanish villagers crushed in a merciless attack by the German air force.

Social movements in the 1930s moved many American artists to become involved with political and moral issues. It was during this period that painter Ben Shahn assaulted the American judicial system in the now-famous painting entitled *The Passion of Sacco and Vanzetti* (1931–1932). Convinced that two immigrants had been convicted and executed by a legal process that was moved more by prejudice against immigrants than by a commitment to justice, Shahn the artist took his stand. The resulting painting, motivated by a personal act of conscience, grew to give form to the feelings of an entire generation.

174

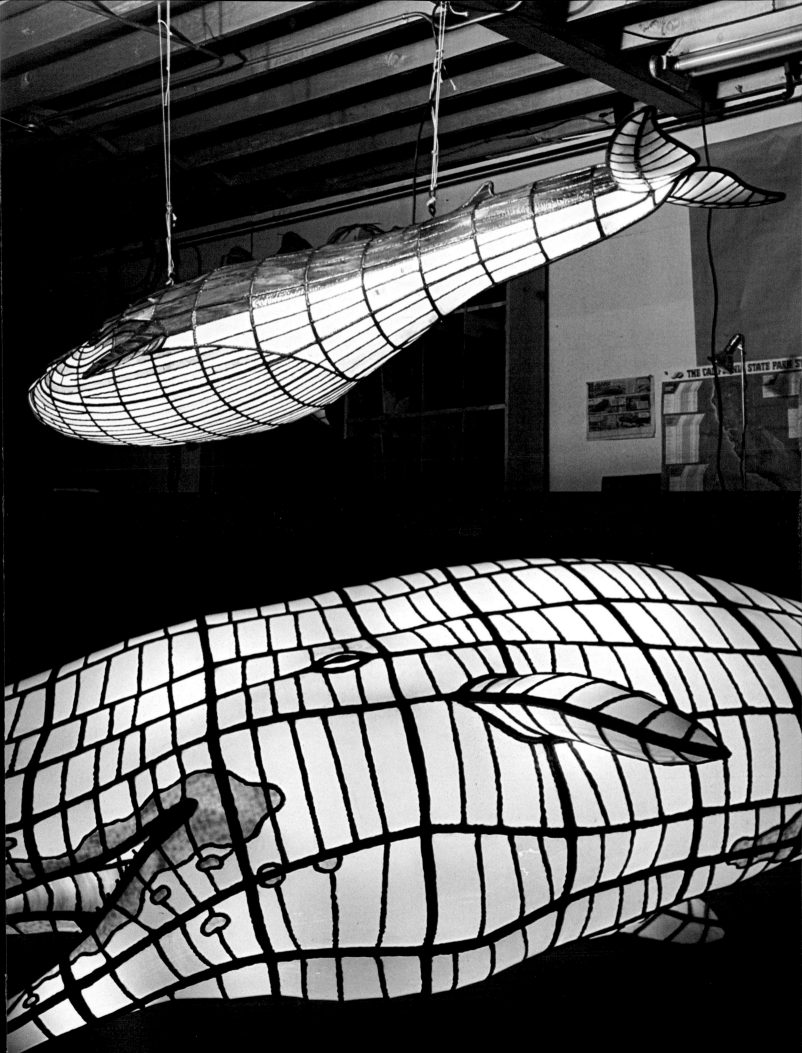

176

177

175

175. *Oxygen Belt.* Pendant. Mary Ann Scherr. 1970. Sterling silver, amber, photocell for oxygen mask and cylinder. Oxygen mask container: 2½″ x 6″. Photograph by Doug Moore.

176. *Heart-Pulse Sensor Bracelet.* Mary Ann Scherr. 1969. Gold and sterling silver. Cuff: 3½″. Photograph by Doug Moore.

177. *Machine #18.* Gary S. Griffin. 1973. Sterling silver and polyester resin. 6″ x 6″ x 6″.

178. *Pendant ⅜-24.* Gary S. Griffin. 1973. Teflon, aluminum, brass, and delrin. H. 5″.

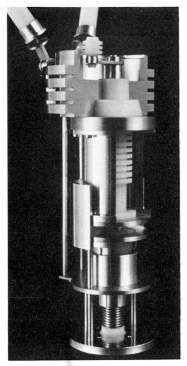

178

Today's advocates have experienced contemporary America's often painful growth into cultural maturity. They have seen Americans themselves grow wealthy in the poverty of an ever more depersonalized society. And they have watched the rich ethnic cultures that blended into the American melting pot being lost forever in a seemingly irreversible assimilation begun two hundred years ago. The advocates are intensely aware of the problems of contemporary America, and they have particular views and comments that they want to share through the vehicle of their work. Some point up the need for social and political reforms. Others seek to formulate expressions rooted in particular ethnic histories and sensibilities. All work with their hands to form a visual "voice" on subjects that have true cultural significance in America today.

California's Larry Foster is a craftsman crusading against the uncontrolled killing of the great whales. Foster, working under the professional name of "General Whale," is outraged that no one has ever even bothered to study the great blue whale alive. He has researched every photograph and measurement available on the great blues to assist in his creation of a group of moody, monochromatic drawings that attempt to depict the great sea mammals that face extinction at the hands of human pursuers who have never even bothered to photograph them in their natural ocean home. Foster uses the drawings as the basis for printing a wide range of posters and mailers that he circulates to attract support for "Save the Whale" campaigns all across the country.

Along with his drawing and printing, Foster finds time to create impressive life-size leaded-glass whales. These fantastic constructions are illuminated internally. They radiate a brilliant light that is dramatically crosshatched with the patterns of the delicate lead strips that support the glass and give the sculpture its form. Foster's glass leviathans glow with mystery. They seem to be the ghosts of all the great whales that have been so needlessly and thoughtlessly exterminated. As an artist, Foster has made powerful use of the deflated forms of death as reminders of the fragility of life. His drawings and his glass constructions are urgent visual messages protesting the imminent extinction of the largest of all earth's creatures. Traveling the country in a special van with a life-size 5,000-pound ferro-cement California gray whale that he built to dramatize his cause, Foster is a craftsman with a mission.

179

179. *Pendant with Carved Face*. Charles Loloma. 1973. Sand-cast gold and blue turquoise. H. 4″. Photograph by K. J. McCullough. (Private collection)

180. *Two Gold Bracelets*. Charles Loloma. 1973. Sandstone cast with inlaid blue turquoise; ironwood, fossil ivory, lapis, coral, and turquoise. (Left) H. 3″; W. 1″. (Right) H. 2¼″; W. 1½″.

181. Bracelet. Charles Loloma. 1976. Construction and inlay in gold and Mourinci turquoise. 2½″ x ¾″. Photograph by K. J. McCullough. (Private collection)

Many issues involving man and his technological environment have become very real today. While government and industry argue endlessly over causes and effects, Americans must drink water of dubious purity, breathe exhaust fumes in their city streets, and overstress their hearts in the all too familiar "rat racet." Ohio jeweler Mary Ann Scherr has stepped to the fore of the craftsmen actively seeking to provide modern man with some real relief from his thoroughly modern problems.

Hoping that her jewelry can save lives, Scherr works in collaboration with doctors and scientists to create handsome new craft forms that provide a broad range of new services. Among her recent creations is a bracelet with a pulse sensor that marks the wearer's heartbeat with a small blinking light. The bracelet electronically notes any sudden change in a pulse and sets off a warning buzzer to alert the wearer of danger. Another Scherr idea led to the production of an air-pollution-monitoring pendant that contains a small oxygen mask. The pendant indicates excessive pollution levels and the mask will provide ten minutes of oxygen for the wearer, who should need no further prompting to head for a locale with cleaner air.

Each of Scherr's pieces is intended to be as aesthetically interesting as it is serviceable. Her work is beautifully crafted in a variety of materials ranging from stainless steel to precious metals and ivory. The possibilities inherent in life-monitoring jewelry may have great impact in the near future as craftsmen like Mary Ann Scherr continue to explore a new art specifically intended to serve as a tangible advocacy of life itself.

Living high on an Arizona mesa in the desert village of Hotevilla, jeweler Charles Loloma creates craft forms that are evolved directly from his Hopi heritage. Loloma, the advocate, is a critical link between contemporary America and the rich indigenous Indian culture of her past. Incorporating the colors and textures of the Arizona landscape into jewelry forms based on traditional Hopi designs, Loloma keeps the lore and wisdom of the Southwestern Indian alive. Loloma's intense involvement with ethnic identity in his work is reflected in his philosophy of art. He says: ". . . it's just not on the surface. This is not a simplified thing . . . there's a lot of thought into it. There's music, there's great dance form that is taking place. These are the things you realize, and then the music becomes the jewelry" (Wesley Holden, "What You See Is a Lot of Soul," *Arizona Highways,* August 1974, p. 6).

183

182

154

182. *Club Vase*. Michael Frimkess. 1965. Ceramic; bisque fired to Cone 05 with china-paint overglaze. H. 36". Photograph courtesy Arthur Bloomenfield. (Arthur Bloomenfield)

183. *Blues for Dr. Banks*. Covered jar. Michael Frimkess. 1975. Ceramic, white ground with china-paint overglaze. H. 24". Photograph by Lou Frimkess. (Dr. Leon Banks)

In Loloma's view fine craft work, like people, must possess some hidden beauty. Each of his works is a masterful demonstration of craftsmanship in turquoise, silver, gold, ivory, and wood. Each of his compositions has a special harmony of form and proportion. For Charles Loloma, life and art fuse together to link a particular cultural past to one artist's view of the future. He marks his works with this identity and in the process finds an expression filled with the dignity and optimism of his Indian birthright.

For many craftsmen, machines often symbolize an impersonal environment, the separation of life and work, and the boredom of assembly-line production. Metalworker Gary S. Griffin steadfastly refuses to accept this narrow viewpoint. To him, shapes made by machines and even machines themselves are as compelling as the shapes that come from nature. The machine is critical to Griffin's work. His jewelry and tiny sculptures are made with comparatively little handwork. He uses machine processes and machine parts to illustrate that there is beauty in technology and that man can learn to work with machines for humanistic solutions to the problems of the future.

Griffin's metal pieces incorporate turned forms fashioned on the lathe in concert with planar volumes shaped at a milling machine. He uses the cool natural colors of machine-finished metals to increase the systemic qualities that he seeks in his art. In each piece, Griffin is able to orchestrate shapes and colors into a rhythm that simulates the sensual, driving pulse of mechanized technology. Griffin's precise and elegant metalworks are effective advocates for his philosophy that machines should be understood and properly used by artists and scientists alike, not for fragmentation, but for creation. As an artist, Griffin makes it apparent that the curves and angles of a mechanical gear can be as beautiful as those of a chambered nautilus.

184. *Things Ain't What They Used to Be*. Covered jar. Michael Frimkess. 1965. Ceramic; bisque fired to Cone 05 with china-paint overglaze. H. 37¾″. Photograph by Leonard Nadel. (Museum of Contemporary Crafts, Johnson Wax Collection)

185. *Ecology Krater*. Michael Frimkess. 1976. Ceramic, stoneware with china-paint overglaze. H. 26″. Photograph by Lou Frimkess. (James Willis Gallery, San Francisco)

Potter Michael Frimkess has been working in clay for twenty years. His art attitudes evolved from an early association with the Funk movement, where he discovered his personal sympathy for creative statements rooted in dissension. Today he is deeply committed to a political cause involving international peace and human understanding. Like Thomas Nast and Herblock, Frimkess has discovered the political potential of cartoon satire. His classic vessel forms are covered with comic-strip friezes complete with "speech balloons" that lampoon the problems of segregation, corruption, and hypocrisy. Frimkess is outspoken in his belief that the primary role of an artist is to demonstrate visually the possibilities for an audience that must confront the work and grow as a result of the confrontation. Speaking of his pottery, he said in an interview with the author, "I want the work to be something—something that someone sees and finds as a beginning for them."

Racial strife is a dominant theme in Frimkess's work. He feels that America must end racial tensions as the first step toward real peace. Using bright, low-fire glazes, he "peoples" his surfaces with red, yellow, black, and white figures endlessly embroiled in the foibles of life. Nothing is sacred to Frimkess: his cartoon superman raises his hand in a stiff Nazi salute; his half-nude Uncle Sam chases an interracial trio of girls down the street. There is little doubt that Frimkess feels that it will take more than superheroes and political figureheads to right the injustices he sees around him.

Even in his most pensive moods Frimkess hits hard. His incredible *Ecology Krater* (1976) falls back on ancient Greek forms to broadcast a very modern message. The krater vessel itself is perfectly thrown and decorated in the traditional black and red of its Greek antecedent. The red figures, however, are modern Americans pedaling a continuous bicycle around the jar. Their efforts somehow seem both to support and to frustrate the common good. Above their heads the artist has painted a delicate frieze that enshrines each of the world's endangered species of animals. The bison, the rhinoceros, the bald eagle, and the rest all seem to wait for the distracted humans below to decide their fate.

Depicting situations that vividly point up the inequities of our social system, Michael Frimkess is a necessary and healthy part of an open society. His work functions as a "gadfly" that continually prods our often cumbersome social institutions and our frequently lethargic social sensibilities. Frimkess, the advocate, is resolute in his stance. When asked why he has committed his creativity to a cause, he replied in an interview with the author: "It is what keeps me going—otherwise I would have quit [potting] long ago."

184

185

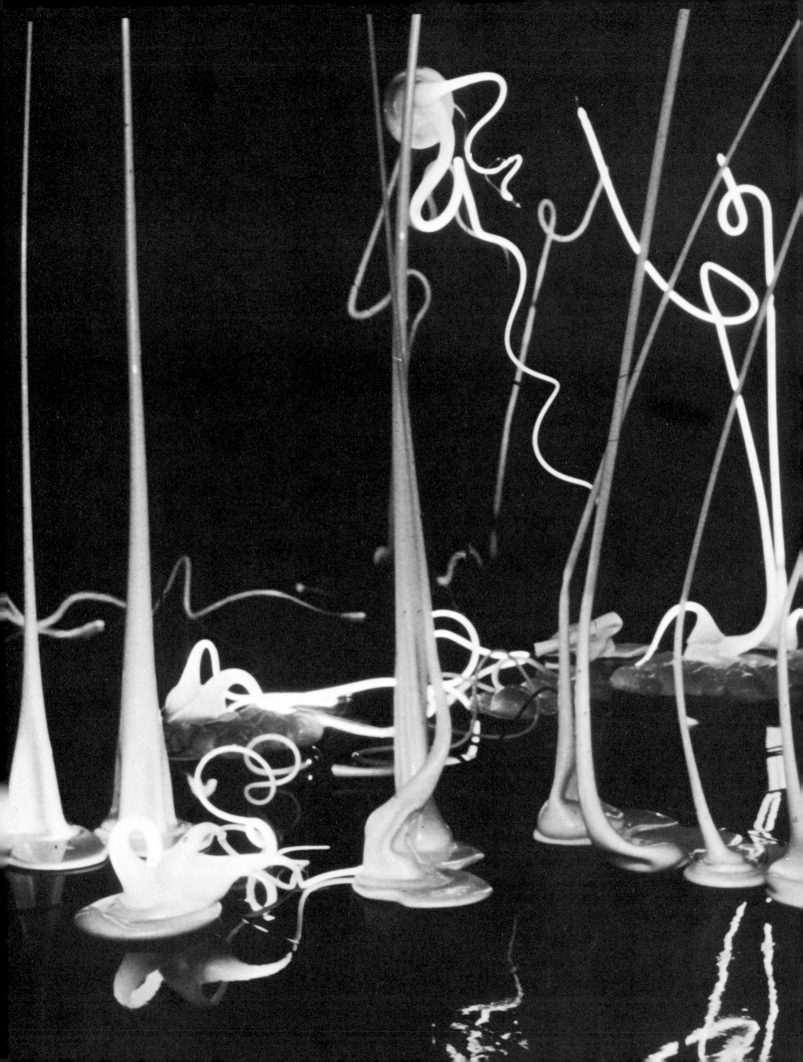

IN PUBLIC SPACES

Blunk
Chihuly and Carpenter
Cook
De Staebler
Duckworth
Grossen
Hicks
Knodel
Paley

186. *Glass Environment.*
Dale Chihuly and James
Carpenter. 1971. Glass and
neon. 18′ x 40′. (Museum
Bellerive, Zurich)

187. Wrought-iron fence for the Hunter Museum of Art (in progress). Albert Paley. 1976. L. 85'; H. 13½'. Photograph by David Darby. (Hunter Museum of Art, Chattanooga, Tennessee)

188. Gates for Renwick Gallery, Smithsonian Institution. Albert Paley. 1975. H. 90½"; W. 72". Photograph by R. Arnold. (Smithsonian Institution, Washington, D.C.)

Over the past two decades a new, ambitious, public, and truly monumental craft expression has emerged on the American scene to complement the more private, personal, and intimate production that has traditionally defined the craft idiom. This renaissance in monumental crafts is decidedly an urban phenomenon stimulated by the scale of urban spaces. Modern high-rise buildings, shopping malls, public plazas, and civic centers have all called for the humanizing touch of the craftsman. In response, contemporary ceramists, woodworkers, metalsmiths, and particularly fiber artists are creating works of sufficient size and presence to hold their own in the contemporary urban environment. Working from different points of origin and often from different perspectives, this group of craftsmen can, nonetheless, be appropriately called the *monumentalists*.

The ambition to create monumental art is age-old. Ancient civilizations aggrandized their deities, their leaders, and their notable buildings with imposing works of sculpture, frescoes, and mosaics. The pyramids of Egypt, the great buddhas of India, and the Sistine ceiling are all part of this tradition. Craftsmen have figured prominently in the construction of many of history's most famous monuments. Master stonecutters fashioned Angkor Wat and the Parthenon. The famous Unicorn tapestries in Cluny and the magnificent stained-glass windows of Bourges Cathedral came from the hands of the finest craftsmen of medieval Europe.

There is a basic relationship between architecture and monumental art. Historically, architects have been the primary patrons of craftsmen working at monumental scale. Unfortunately, their patronage has been sporadic and undependable for contemporary American craftsmen. Only as

187

189. Tapestry commissioned for the Embarcadero Center, San Francisco. Lia Cook. 1975. Wool, cotton, jute, and foam rubber. H. 36'; W. 12'. Photograph courtesy Allrich Gallery. (Embarcadero Center)

190. Tapestry (detail). Lia Cook. 1975. Wool, cotton, jute, and foam rubber. H. 36'; W. 12'. Photograph courtesy Allrich Gallery. (Embarcadero Center)

191. *Tassajara.* Bench (one of a grouping of 12 pieces). J. B. Blunk. 1974. Redwood (1,400 years old). L. 96". Photograph by J. B. Blunk. (Tassajara Zen Mountain Center)

the American urban environment faced the full threat of being swallowed up by the cold efficiency of advanced engineering and technology have architects found a place for the work of the craftsman.

From its inception in the 1930s, the International Style of architecture purged itself of all forms of adornment that were not direct outgrowths of the structure of a building itself. This view disenfranchised many craftsmen who had traditionally supported themselves creating architectural pieces. Drifting away from collaboration with architects, the American craftsman became increasingly involved with "art for art's sake." The independence gained by the crafts during this period proved the ability of the craft movement to survive on its own. More importantly, it facilitated the growth of independent new forms of crafts.

By the 1960s, however, directions in both architecture and the crafts made a rapprochement between them inevitable. As mature coequals, the two arts have come together in a relationship that is truly symbiotic. The expansive clean white walls of modern building design are an excellent showplace for the spectrum of bold colors and variegated textures of contemporary fiber work. Open geometric foyers and lobbies are greatly enriched by the organic quality of fired clay, and the austere planarity of contemporary walls

191

189

190

often welcomes the contrast of hand-forged iron. For the craftsman today, the spaces and planes of modern buildings become points of departure—the impetus for the creation of new works that can harmoniously complement or radically restructure architecture.

Within the last few years, Rochester, New York, artist-craftsman Albert Paley has been commissioned to create monumental gates and fences for major museums around the country. Each of Paley's iron pieces, such as the superb gates for the Renwick Gallery (1975) of the Smithsonian Institution in Washington, D.C., is hand-fashioned using the traditional craft of the blacksmith. His fence for the sculpture courtyard for the Hunter Museum (1976) in Chattanooga, Tennessee, is eighty-five feet long and thirteen feet high. In all of these gates and fences, the inherently rigid nature of iron is belied by the artist's masterful handling of his medium. Within the rigor of a fence line, Paley has been able to draw freely in space with an unyielding material in which he has discovered an almost plastic essence. His work is characterized by a pulsing concert of lines and curves that often crescendo in a pair of heroic gates. Sophisticated and beautifully crafted, these Paley constructions soar as a tribute to the skills and ambitions of the new American craftsman.

The environmental wood furniture of J.B. Blunk is chain-saw-carved out of giant California redwood trunks and roots weighing several tons. Blunk enjoys the physical challenge of his work. Each log is studied for its potentials and for its flaws. The wood speaks, and the artist listens. Blunk relies on both instinct and experience to hew his images from the wood. He has made free-form tables, benches, and play sculptures for a park. Each piece is always individual and each is suited to the visual needs of its site. His sprawling organic forms bring a new energy to public spaces and a new interpretation to the concept of functional sculpture.

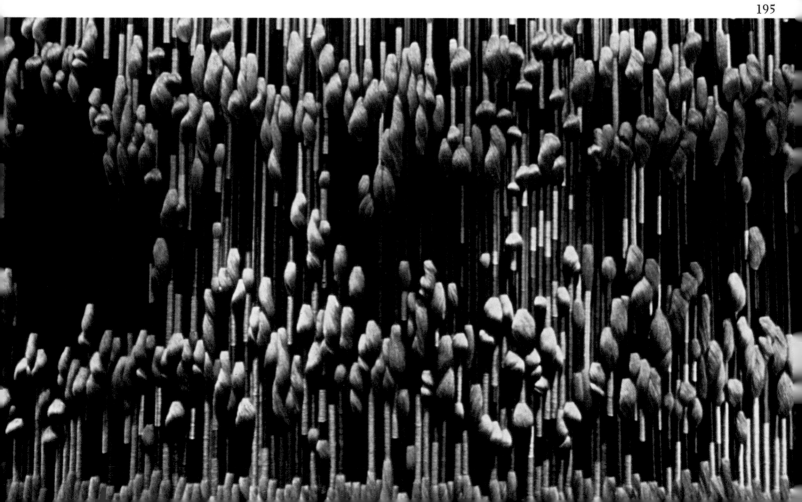

194. *Act 8* (detail). Gerhardt
G. Knodel. 1974. China silk
and nylon cord.

195. *Wall* (detail). Sheila
Hicks. 1970. Natural linens,
wrapped with silk, wood, and
synthetic fiber. 10′ x 16′.
Photograph by Jonas
Dovydenas. (Banque de
Rothschild)

196. *Act 8*. Gerhardt G.
Knodel. 1974. China silk and
nylon cord. 8′ x 10′ x 14′
(when opened); 8′ x 10′ x 20″
(when closed).

196

Stephen De Staebler's gigantic clay constructions
loom from wall surfaces and rumble across floor planes. Set
against the starkness of contemporary architectural interiors,
De Staebler's brooding forms seem to have been displaced
from the site of some ancient geologic upheaval. The clay
itself slumps and folds, buckles and lifts, its surfaces cut
and marked through the process of shaping. The natural
slumped clay contours of his chairs and benches cup the
forms of the human body in repose. They bring to mind
the inviting and restful eroded stone shapes that served
early man as furniture in his first cave dwellings. De
Staebler's work is rich in color effects achieved by rubbing
oxides and pigments into the raw clay. Fired and finished,
this unique furniture adds both visual enrichment and
physical comfort to living spaces. Working clay at a scale
where natural forces constantly conspire to destroy a piece
during drying and firing, De Staebler defies the limits of his
medium in producing monumental works that seem to
bring the outdoors indoors to complement and challenge the
environments they inhabit.

Many of the new monumentalists work in fiber, constructing images that utilize the open form potentials of
the fiber medium. The suspended fabric environments of
Gerhardt Knodel articulate interior spaces with panels
of fabric hung from elaborate monofilament harnesses. The
forms of Knodel's constructions, like sets for a theatre, turn
viewers into actors in highly personal plays involving the
self, the place, and the artist's work.

The scale of Knodel's work is often imposing, but the
experience of each piece is intimate and ephemeral. The
sheer fabric planes are dyed in colors and patterns that interact with the light and the atmosphere in a room, changing
static light into a shimmering illumination filtered through
the overlapping translucent layers of colored fabric. Knodel
is involved with the dichotomy that can exist in fabric and
in form. His fabrics are alternately dark and dry, then

light and shimmering. His colors move from cool to hot, and back again. His woven forms are perceived alternately as shapes ensnared by a reseau of static rhythmic cables, or as free, fluttering, airy configurations of color and pattern. Knodel's work reinforces fabric associations that he feels are common in everyone's experience. His panels and canopies are always folded and draped with systemic and sculptural precision.

Commissioned monumental art imposes particular problems and restrictions on its creators. Interactions with clients, engineers, architects, and interior decorators are a given in the equation. Budgets, financing, and the complex logistics of installations are constant problems. Monumentalists must plan each step of their installation and anticipate future maintenance perfectly, since mistakes at architectural scale can be disastrous. They must visualize a large work while working on a small model or sketch. Many forms are not always successful at large scale, even though they make a very interesting maquette. The light, space, and even foot traffic of a site must be completely taken into account to ensure an optimum integration of art and architecture. Despite the complexities and difficulties, more and more craftsmen are enjoying the realization of their concepts at heroic scale.

Lia Cook works in the tradition of monumental tapestry. Her commission installed at the Embarcadero Center (1975) in San Francisco vividly illustrates the way in which contemporary art can enrich an architectural site without losing its integrity as art. Cook's brightly colored woven geometric field rises up two stories high along one wall of the center. From afar the tapestry has a dramatic painterly impact; up close its weight and texture become decidedly sculptural. Cook's innovational technique of compressing thick strips of plastic foam in the weft of her weaving traps a turgid, physical life-force in the basic structure of the tapestry itself. Like all tapestry makers, Cook deals practically with the realization that the whole of her art is made up of the sum of its parts. The beauty and monumentality of her work grows out of her careful and expert handling of the strand-by-strand construction of everything she creates.

A native of Switzerland, Françoise Grossen has lived and worked for many years in the United States, creating large weavings for public spaces. Grossen utilizes hand-dyed Manila hemp in much of her work, celebrating the beauty of rugged, unpretentious materials. Her wall hangings drape in easy curves lifted by a few taut vertical cords. Within the folds of her weavings, many varieties of knotting techniques alter the surface texture. Small macrame knots flow into large thick convoluted twists. These textural changes cause swells of movement within the structure of the fabric itself, freeing counterpoints of rhythmic patterns. One of the most outstanding aspects of Grossen's oeuvre is her masterly and sensitive use of color. Like Gauguin, she exploits the

197. *La Mémoire.* Sheila Hicks. 1972. Natural linen, wool, and synthetic fibers. 121″ x 176″. (IBM, Paris)

198. *Earth, Water, and Sky.* Ruth Duckworth. 1968. Ceramic. 8′10″ x 11′. (Geophysical Sciences Building, University of Chicago)

197

198

199. *U.S. #2.* Françoise Grossen. 1970. Sisal. 96" x 120". (Mrs. Jacob M. Kaplan)

pure force of exquisite color in her art. Her purplish-blues and primitive oranges unite the differentiated systems and themes that wander through her weaving. Grossen's tapestries bring an urgent beauty to any environment.

Few fiber workers are more experienced in working with public spaces than Sheila Hicks. An inveterate traveler with a prodigious appetite for work, Hicks has traversed the world over the past decade, creating fiber walls for a growing international patronage of corporations and private collectors. Throughout her travels, Hicks has gained an impressive insight into the multifaceted history of fiber and human culture. From Mexico to India and Chile, she has studied ancient and contemporary fiber-working techniques and has distilled her own personal commitment to fiber structures from this study.

Hicks's fiber wall (1969) for the executive suite of the Banque de Rothschild in Paris is one of the major fiber monuments of the past decade. The wall is constructed of thick, wrapped yarn bundles that hang side by side from ceiling to floor. Each cluster of raw linen threads is tightly wrapped with lustrous silk fibers. The wrapping is stopped at several points along each bundle to allow the raw linen to balloon out of the constricting silk sheath. The wrapping silk fibers throughout the piece have been dyed in a range of blue tones that varies from near-black to brilliant turquoise. These contrast exquisitely with the natural buffs of the exposed linen. Side by side, these colored sculptured tubes create a dense curtain plane that undulates physically and visually with ripples of color and texture expanding in cloudlike patterns. At huge scale, the wall becomes a skyscape or an undersea world—a monument to the sensory and aesthetic dimensions of one craftsman's artistry.

The contemporary craftsman's approach to monumental work is singular. In a time when so many large fountains and sculptures for public spaces are being constructed by commercial fabrication shops, the majority of craftsmen still prefer to do their own work. The craftsman is justifiably hesitant about assuming the role of a pure designer, when so much of what is beautiful and important about contemporary craft work springs directly from the craftsman's personal touch. It is this life that is needed in today's public spaces. The monumentalists, true to their craft traditions, believe that life flows directly from the mind, spirit, and hand into the shaping of materials into form. The monumental, thus, presents a unique challenge to the craftsman who, fully aware of the personal work and commitment involved, accepts large public commissions. Somehow it all seems worth it every time a new work goes into place. The quality of American life becomes a little richer, and the scope of contemporary culture a little broader—the craftsman and the public could ask for little more.

200. Barbara Shawcroft's studio-living quarters in Berkeley, California.

201. Arthur Carpenter in front of his studio in Bolinas, California.

202. Contemporary quilt exhibition, Los Angeles County Museum of Art, California, 1976.

203. Peter Voulkos at a workshop at the University of Kentucky, Lexington, Kentucky.

200

201

THE CRAFTSMAN'S WORLD

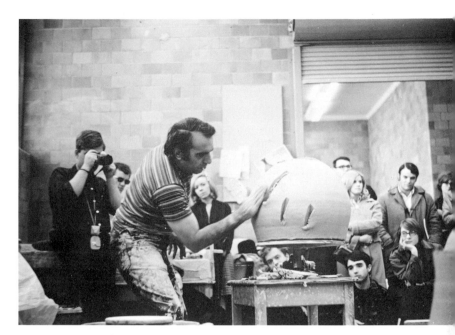

203

202

The contemporary craftsman's world is busy and mobile. Nevertheless, it revolves around a few basic constants. Work as a way of life is the most fundamental aspect of the craftsman's world. Whereas most of the world works to live, the craftsman lives to work. There is something basic in the work traditions of all the craft disciplines that becomes a life rhythm, a pulse that sustains the potter, the weaver, the metal- or woodworker, and the glassblower through the seasons, year in and year out.

William Morris understood the work demands of the craftsman's life and believed that there was something ennobling to be found in this life for the enlightened modern artists who would turn their talents and temperaments to it. Most of today's craftsmen share this belief and recognize the commitment to work as one of the fundamental bonds joining the craft community together in a strong sense of its own identity.

Craftsmen enjoy the routine of work. They approach their work as a process or cycle that becomes a sort of clock around which they pace their lives. No craftsman spends one hundred percent of his or her time in the throes of creation. The craftsman's creative impulse is sustained and nourished by work processes involving a certain amount of routine. This routine provides rest and rejuvenation for the mind and spirit while keeping the hands and body tuned to the rhythms of ongoing productivity. Each discipline has its repetitive or arduous aspects that attend and support the creative process. Potters spend hours mixing clay and monitoring the drying of their pottery. Weavers are perpetually dyeing yarns or setting up their looms for the next length of fabric to be woven. A metalsmith raising a bowl expends thousands of hammerblows simply to rough out a form. A woodworker puts a major effort into the selection and curing of wood before it is ever used, and then expends many more hours of labor sanding and finishing a piece after its form has been shaped. Professional craftsmen find pleasure and satisfaction in all aspects of their work. Those who do not will not remain professionals for long.

Many craftsmen incorporate teaching into their work schedules. Proud of their skills and eager to impart them to the next generation, teaching craftsmen meet the challenge of instruction with the same patience and dedication with which they pursue their art. Across America today, many craftsmen have become high-ranking tenured members of university faculties. The academic community has increasingly recognized the value of aesthetic disciplines and has come to depend on the input of teaching craftsmen as a measure of what is truly human in the curricular area of the humanities.

The life of the craftsman also frequently includes a

204. Neda Al-Hilali, Venice, California.

205. Paul Soldner, Aspen, Colorado.

206. George Nakashima, New Hope, Pennsylvania.

204

205

206

considerable amount of travel. School and community workshops invite craftsmen from different locales to demonstrate their skills and to lecture on their work and their point of view. Workshops keep the craft world in touch with itself. From studio to studio or campus to campus, ideas move quickly and directly. The creative cross-pollination that results from this fluid interaction of the craft community is vital to the health of the crafts today. The exposure of frequent travel has transformed the American craftsman from a provincial tradesman into a mobile urbane artist—comfortable and productive in both rustic and urban situations.

At home, the craftsman's world is a personal environment completely shaped to suit individual needs. Today's craftsmen transform urban warehouse spaces into well-lit studios and luxurious living quarters. Others renovate farms, turning barns into inviting studio or showroom spaces, and remodeling early frame houses to fit contemporary life-styles. Still others go even further. Starting from the ground up, they build studios and homes that become provocative experimental expressions of handmade architecture.

Individuality is the key to the craftsman's environment. Furnishings and even details of door latches and lighting are particularized to the needs and taste of each artist. Many craftsmen trade works between themselves and live in the midst of a veritable museum of beautiful artworks. The craftsman's sense of roots and tradition is often expressed in a taste for studios and homes filled with antiques, hand-finished architectural details, and the lushness of growing plants. The sense of life is everywhere. Pets abound, and gardens flourish. The new American craftsman celebrates life in a world filled with the textures of handmade furniture, the brilliant colors of flowers and wall hangings, and the smells of herbs, spices, and foods in preparation.

The professional craftsmen meet the public through exhibitions and craft fairs. The craft fair is an updated version of a public market, complete with rows of portable stalls where craftsmen display and sell their work. A contemporary craft fair is a well-organized public event generally sponsored by business associations or municipal agencies. A typical fair requires months of planning and culminates in the transformation of several city blocks into a pedestrian mall filled with visitors strolling from booth to booth, talking with artists, and viewing their work.

Many craftsmen seek affiliations with galleries that display and sell their work. For them, exhibitions provide an opportunity to solicit serious critical comment about pieces making their first debut out of the studio. Exhibitions are often the climax of months of work and become festive highlights in the craftsman's year. The public taste in craft-

207. Karen Karnes at her studio in Stony Point, New York.

work has kept pace with the craft vanguard, and openings of new exhibitions are well attended and generally well patronized. A growing number of galleries and museums now schedule group and one-person shows of craftwork. Art associations and museums also frequently sponsor national competitive craft exhibitions where substantial cash and purchase prizes are awarded to works judged most outstanding out of the thousands of objects submitted from all across the country.

The craftsman's world is a world of contrasts. The lifestyles, personalities, and philosophies of the American craftsman are shaped from the broad milieu of the American experience. The attraction of the crafts is obvious. All of the disciplines have long and proud histories. They also offer challenging futures that are open to all who respond to the touch of materials and the satisfaction of creative endeavor. The craftsman comes to his or her calling free. There will always be craftsmen, for there will always be those who will turn their hands to giving form to things yet unshaped and to bringing order to what is seemingly chaotic. The craftsman's eyes and hands see and feel what otherwise remains invisible and intangible. A lump of clay, a skein of yarn, a batch of cullet—transformed—becomes identity—an identity built a day at a time, as each artist explores and extends a talent, an idea, and a skill. A few in each generation find their way into the craftsman's world to live the traditions and to work for the changes that constitute the double inheritance of William Morris. Despite his foresight, it is doubtful that Morris could really have foreseen the craftsman's world as it is today, but he sensed the enduring value of creative people and would have been proud to see his bequest being shaped so skillfully by the hands of the new American craftsman.

207

208. J. B. Blunk, Inverness, California.

209. Charles Loloma, Hotevilla, Arizona.

210. Arline Fisch, San Diego, California.

211. Peter Voulkos, Berkeley, California.

212. Trude Guermonprez (1910–1976), San Francisco, California.

213. Al Rice, Berkeley, California.

214. "Dr. Gladstone" and *Hollywood Peckerus Absurdus* near Crockett, California.

210

209

211

212

214

213

215 (Overleaf, page 180).
Glen Zweygardt's hand-built
home in Alfred, New York.

216 (Overleaf, page 181,
top). Paul Soldner's studio
near Aspen, Colorado, with
his experimental solar-heated
house in background.

217 (Overleaf, page 181,
bottom). J. B. Blunk's garden
outside his home in the
mountains near Inverness,
California.

218. Gary Noffke's unique
house during its construction.

219. Outside the studio of
Studebaker buff Clayton
Bailey in Crockett, California.

220 (Overleaf, page 184).
Stanley Lechtzin in his
studio in Philadelphia,
Pennsylvania.

221 (Overleaf, pages 184–
185). Woodworking tools,
Espenet Studio, Bolinas,
California.

222 (Overleaf, page 185).
Unloading Jun Kaneko's kiln
in Providence, Rhode Island.

218

223 (Overleaf, page 186).
Arthur Carpenter's studio
in Bolinas, California.

224 (Overleaf, pages 186–
187). Greenware in Betty
Woodman's studio in
Boulder, Colorado.

225 (Overleaf, page 187).
Albert Paley at his forge in
Rochester, New York.

226. A student learning the
potter's craft at the Hinckley
School of Crafts, Deer Isle,
Maine.

227. Exhibition of glass
cylinders by Dale Chihuly,
James Yaw Gallery,
Birmingham, Michigan.

228

227

229

230

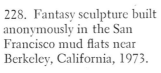
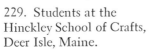

228. Fantasy sculpture built anonymously in the San Francisco mud flats near Berkeley, California, 1973.

229. Students at the Hinckley School of Crafts, Deer Isle, Maine.

230. George Nakashima's wood-drying shed, New Hope, Pennsylvania.

231. Tom McGlauchlin at a glass workshop at The Cranbrook Academy of Art, Bloomfield Hills, Michigan, 1974.

232. Lenore Tawney in her New York studio.

233. Ann Arbor Craft Fair, Ann Arbor, Michigan.

Bibliography

Books

Albers, Anni. *On Weaving.* Middletown, Conn.: Wesleyan University Press, 1965.

Battcock, Gregory. *Minimal Art: A Critical Anthology.* New York: Dutton Paperbacks, 1968.

Bishop, Robert. *Centuries and Styles of the American Chair, 1640–1970.* New York: E. P. Dutton, 1972.

Christensen, Erwin O. *Primitive Art.* New York: The Viking Press, 1955.

Clark, Robert Judson, ed. *The Arts and Crafts Movement in America 1876–1916.* Princeton, N.J.: Princeton University Press, 1972.

Constantine, Mildred, and Larson, Jack Lenor. *Beyond Craft: The Art of Fabric.* New York, Cincinnati, Toronto, London, and Melbourne: Van Nostrand Reinhold Company, 1973.

Dewey, John. *Art As Experience.* New York: Minton, Balch and Co., 1934.

Eisen, Gustav. *Glass: Its Origin, History, Chronology, Technique, and Classification to the Sixteenth Century.* New York: W. E. Rudge, 1927.

Fales, Martha Gandy. *Early American Silver.* New York: Dutton Paperbacks, 1973.

Fisch, Arline M. *Textile Techniques in Metal for Jewelers, Sculptors, and Textile Artists.* New York: Van Nostrand Reinhold, 1975.

Gloag, John, and Bridgewater, Derek. *Cast Iron in Architecture.* London: George Allen and Unwin Ltd., 1948.

Greenberg, Clement. *Art and Culture: Critical Essays.* Boston: Beacon Press, 1961.

Harvey, Virginia I. *Macrame: The Art of Creative Knotting.* New York: Reinhold Publishing Co., 1967.

Herskovits, Melvin J. *Man and His Works.* New York: Alfred A. Knopf, 1948.

Hornung, Clarence Pearson. *Treasury of American Design.* New York: Harry N. Abrams, 1972.

Kampeer, Fritz, and Beyer, Klaus G. *Glass: A World History.* Greenwich, Conn.: New York Graphic Society, 1967.

Koyama, Fujio. *The Heritage of Japanese Ceramics.* New York, Tokyo, and Kyoto: Weatherhill/Tankosha, 1973.

Leach, Bernard. *A Potters Book.* Holly-by-the-Sea, Fla.: Transatlantic Arts, Inc., 1967.

———.*The Potter's Challenge.* New York: E. P. Dutton, 1975.

Littleton, Harvey K. *Glassblowing: A Search for Form.* New York, Cincinnati, Toronto, London, and Melbourne: A Van Nostrand Reinhold Book, 1971.

Lippard, Lucy R., ed. *Surrealists on Art.* Englewood Cliffs, N.J.: Prentice-Hall, 1970.

Members of the Arts and Crafts Exhibition Society, with a preface by William Morris. *Arts and Crafts Essays.* London & Bombay: Longmans, Green, and Co., 1899.

Müller, Grégoire. *The New Avant Garde: Issues for the Art of the Seventies.* New York: Praeger Publishers, 1972.

Nordness, Lee. *Objects: USA.* New York: The Viking Press, 1970.

Osgood, Cornelius. *The Jug and Related Stoneware of Bennington.* Rutland, Vt.: Charles E. Tuttle Company, 1971.

Paz, Octavio (essay), Plaut, James S. (foreword). *In Praise of Hands.* Greenwich, Conn.: New York Graphic Society, 1974.

Penrose, Roland. *The Sculpture of Picasso.* New York: The Museum of Modern Art, 1967.

Rhodes, Daniel. *Clay and Glazes for the Potter.* Radnor, Pa.: Chilton Book Company, 1957, 1973.

Rose, Barbara. *American Art Since 1900: A Critical History.* New York: F. A. Praeger, 1967.

Rossbach, Ed. *Baskets as Textile Art.* New York: Van Nostrand Reinhold, 1973.

Safford, Carleton L., and Bishop, Robert. *America's Quilts and Coverlets.* New York: E.P. Dutton, 1972.

Thomas, Richard. *Metalsmithing for the Artist-Craftsman.* Philadelphia: Chilton Book Company, 1960.

Tomkins, Calvin, and Editors of Time-Life Books. *The World of Marcel Duchamp.* New York: Time Incorporated, 1966.

Tuchman, Maurice. *American Sculpture of the Sixties.* Los Angeles: Contemporary Art Council, 1967.

Wildenhain, Marguerite. *Pottery: Form and Expression.* New York: American Craftsmen's Council, 1959.

Periodicals

Cavell, Marcia. "Taste and the Moral Sense." *The Journal of Aesthetics and Art Criticism.* American Society for Aesthetics, Cleveland Museum (Fall 1975).

Friedberg, Paul M. "Private Space for Public Use." *Design Quarterly.* Walker Art Center (1970).

Gilford, Lydia. "Glass, The Fifth Black Art." *Craft Horizons* (1950).

Goldin, Amy. "Problems in Folk Art." *Artforum,* (June 1976).

McDevitt, Jan. "The Craftsman in Production: A Frank Discussion of the Rewards and Pitfalls." *Craft Horizons* (1964).

Slivka, Rose. "The Object as Poet." *Craft Horizons* (June 1974).

Catalogues

Applegate, Judith, and Varian, Elayne H. *Art Deco.* New York: Finch College Museum of Art, 1970.

Bober, Harry; Fisch, Arline M.; Herman, Lloyd E.; Woolfenden, William E. *The Goldsmith.* Saint Paul, Minn.: Minnesota Museum of Art, 1974.

Constantine, Mildred, and Selz, Peter. *Art Nouveau: Art and Design at the Turn of the Century.* New York: The Museum of Modern Art, 1959, 1975.

Coplans, John. *Abstract Expressionist Ceramics.* Irvine, Calif.: University of California Press, Irvine Division of Fine Arts, 1966.

Friedman, Martin, and various contributors. *American Indian Art: Form and Tradition.* Minneapolis: Walker Art Center and the Minneapolis Institute of Arts, 1972.

Hall, Michael; Hemphill, Herbert W., Jr.; Kan, Michael; Robbins, Daniel. *Folk Sculpture U.S.A.* Brooklyn, N.Y.: The Brooklyn Museum, 1976.

Kester, Bernard, and Wight, Frederick S. *Deliberate Entanglements.* Los Angeles: University of California Press, 1971.

Luck, Robert H. *Forms in Metal: 275 Years of Metalsmithing in America.* New York: Museum of Contemporary Crafts-Finch College Museum of Art, 1975.

Perrot, Paul N.; Gardner, Paul V.; Plaut, James S. *Steuben: Seventy Years of American Glassmaking.* New York and Washington: Praeger Publishers, 1974.

Phillips, Rovert F., and Smith, Paul. *American Glass Now.* Toledo, Ohio: The Toledo Museum of Art, 1972.

Selz, Peter. *Funk.* Berkeley, Calif.: University of California Press, 1967.

Smith, Paul. *Sculpture in Fiber.* New York: Museum of Contemporary Crafts, 1972.

Taylor, Joshua C. *Wooden Works.* Saint Paul, Minn.: Smithsonian Institution and the Minnesota Museum of Art, 1972.

Thompson, Robert Farris. *African Art in Motion.* Berkeley and Los Angeles, Calif.: U.C.L.A. Art Council, 1974.

Index

DAT